Praise for *Make More, Worry Less*

"These principles will not only help you sleep at night, they're steroids for your paycheck. This book is a can't miss if you want economic freedom without having to start your own business!"

—**Barbara Babbit Kaufman**, Founder and Former CEO of Chapter 11 Book Stores

"As the owner of a rapidly growing global brand, our business success hinges upon employees who are willing to take the ball and run with it! If you're a business owner or executive responsible for team results, these principles will have people knocking over walls for you!"

—**Giovanni**, The Margarita King Owner and Founder of The Margarita King, www.themargaritaking.com

"As an entrepreneur and former Wall St. investment manager, this book is easy to relate to for anyone who has ever thought about starting their own company, but just never had the 'perfect idea.' Until that perfect idea arrives, this book provides the secret of blending what's great about corporate America with the highlights of business ownership."

—**Kwame Jackson**, *Apprentice* Season 1 Finalist, Entrepreneur/ Speaker/Author, www.kwamejackson.com

"What a cool concept! Moss shows how you can find a balance between working for someone and working for yourself. It's the best of both worlds! I don't care what level you are at work—you can start today!"

—**Allison Saget**, Author of *The Event Marketing Handbook*, www.eventblt.com

"Finally someone has just come out and said it…you can still get rich working for a big company! Moss shows you the way, no matter what industry you're in!"

—**Katherine Vessenes**, CFP JD President of Vestment Advisors

"This is a great concept! As an entrepreneur, I know how hard it is to start a business from the ground up. This book reveals the secrets to business ownership without having to start from scratch. Moss has become quite an inspiration on this topic"

—**Jen Klair**, Founder of www.jenklairkids.com

MAKE MORE,
WORRY LESS

MAKE MORE,
WORRY LESS

Secrets from 18 Extraordinary People Who
Created a Bigger Income and a Better Life

Wes Moss

Vice President, Publisher: Tim Moore
Associate Publisher and Director of Marketing: Amy Neidlinger
Acquisitions Editor: Martha Cooley
Editorial Assistant: Pamela Boland
Development Editor: Russ Hall
Digital Marketing Manager: Julie Phifer
Marketing Coordinator: Megan Colvin
Cover Designer: Chuti Prasertsith
Managing Editor: Gina Kanouse
Senior Project Editor: Kristy Hart
Copy Editor: Bart Reed
Proofreader: Language Logistics, LLC
Indexer: Lisa Stumpf
Compositor: Jake McFarland
Manufacturing Buyer: Dan Uhrig

Printed in the United States of America

First Printing January 2008

ISBN-10:   0-13-234686-9
ISBN-13:   978-0-13-234686-3

Pearson Education LTD.
Pearson Education Australia PTY, Limited.
Pearson Education Singapore, Pte. Ltd.
Pearson Education North Asia, Ltd.
Pearson Education Canada, Ltd.
Pearson Educatión de Mexico, S.A. de C.V.
Pearson Education—Japan
Pearson Education Malaysia, Pte. Ltd.

Moss, Wes.
  Make more, worry less : 18 rules for a bigger income and a better life / Wesley Moss.
    p. cm.
  ISBN 0-13-234686-9 (hbk. : alk. paper) 1. Career development. 2. Job satisfaction. 3. Success in business. I. Title.
  HF5381.M747 2008
  332.024'01—dc22
                          2007035339

This book is dedicated to my wife Lynne,
son Ben, and our growing family.

*May we make more of our future
and worry less of tomorrow.*

Contents

Acknowledgments

I used to say that writing a book was a male's version of having a baby. Then in the middle of working on this project my wife and I actually had a baby—our first. I was there from the very beginning all the way through labor—and I no longer relate writing a book to having a child. Writing a book is much easier, and I'd take it any day over morning sickness, 24 hours of contractions, and delivery—especially delivery! We are now blessed with a baby boy named Ben, and I realize that parenthood is the coolest thing in the world.

In the meantime I'd like to thank my wife Lynne who has already proven to be a tremendous mother and advocate for my work. She has endured many a sleepless night so that I could be fresh for work the next day and has kept our household running strong despite countless book deadlines and Sunday morning radio shows. Ben is a lucky kid.

Work

I work at a big company, actually a huge company—one of the largest investment firms in the world. Despite their conservative nature and responsibility for more than seventy thousand employees, the structure is nimble enough to support my efforts as a financial advisor, an author, and radio host. It says a great deal about the people in charge. So in that same vein, I would like to thank Jerry Johnson and his charming and supportive staff. Jerry is the ultimate example of how someone can find extraordinary success as an entrepreneur and as an employee in the corporate world.

I would also like to thank the people I work with on a daily basis:

Steve Meadows for always helping me to "worry less" and encouraging me to "make more."

Dan Moss and Tim Jeffrey for being extraordinary business partners—the three of us have been through a great deal together, and I could not be blessed with two more honest and genuinely good people to work with. I appreciate their continued input, creativity, support, and hard work as we continue to expand our wealth management practice together.

Jenna Hooton, my famous client service associate who keeps the engine running smoothly, keeps our clients happy, and ensures that I'm the most organized and efficient person in Atlanta.

Ryan Ely for being an intern mogul—from running spreadsheets for investment analysis, to brainstorming on concepts for this book, to helping produce my investment radio show—this kid gives students at Georgia Tech a good name.

Outside of Work

The following people are truly one in a million:

Judy Potwora, who has been an extraordinary partner on this project—I thank her for her coolness under pressure, her creativity under fire, and her ability to make the impossible happen. I'm thankful every day for having met her and having the opportunity to work with her.

Lilian Raji of the Lilian Raji Agency, who is one of the few PR people in Atlanta not afraid to get into the trenches and get things done. I thank her for her diligence and persistence.

Jon Maylsiak, my version of Jerry Maguire, who is always looking out for me and finding the right people to work with.

The right people to work with: FT Press. Thank you Martha and Tim for believing in my quest to help people really "make more" of anything, and "worry less" about everything.

Lastly I would like to thank all of the amazing participants interviewed for this book. Thank you for your valuable insights and for breathing life into this project! I am eternally grateful.

About the Author

Wes Moss is the host of "The Wes Moss Show" and is an actively practicing Certified Financial Planner in Atlanta, Georgia. His goal is to help his listeners and clients make smarter financial decisions on a daily basis. He and his partners manage nearly a quarter of a billion dollars in investments for people much like you. He is also the author of *Starting from Scratch—Secrets from 21 Ordinary People Who Made the Entrepreneurial Leap*. For audiences who are ready to learn and have a blast, Wes delivers keynote speeches titled the "Entrepreneur Within" and "Make More of *Anything*, Worry Less about *Everything*."

For more information about Wes Moss, go to his website, www.wesmoss.com.

Introduction

Think back for a minute to the last time you had a restless night sleep. What was racing through your brain? Typically what keeps people up, tossing and turning, is worry about control—the control they have of their future. If you're lying awake at night, it's likely because you feel insecure about something. You're probably worried about taking care of your family, paying bills, advancing at your job, getting your kids through college, and on top of it all—saving for retirement!

These are all big nuts to crack and can all be huge points of anxiety. The pharmaceutical industry has made billions off of anxiety meds trying to help people calm down. The biggest stress that lies at the root of our security—or insecurity? Ownership! Ownership of your career, ownership of your job, ownership over the amount of money you make, and ownership over your future. Ownership over your career means more time and more money for the things that you want to do for yourself and your family. Have control and ownership at work—and your days filled with worry will be numbered.

I know a lot about worry. I work in financial planning, an industry at the mercy of the financial markets. My first few years on the job I saw the Standard and Poor's 500 Index drop 45 percent in two years. In those days I learned that worries about money and security can lead to more worries. Luckily, early on I read Dale Carnegie's *How to Stop Worrying and Start Living* and noticed how worry perpetuates itself. That's because when we worry we undermine our inner security and feel more insecure; and, when we're insecure, we're not likely to take ownership of our own lives and careers. So we end up in a cycle of worry and indecision that undercuts our ability to get the most out of life. The cure for indecision is clarity, which I found with help from some great mentors. This book is full of examples of people who overcame indecision and worry, took ownership of their careers, and found more security. They can be great mentors for you.

Make More

The people in this book are each very different, but what they all have in common is that they didn't sit back and have promotions fall in their laps. They're normal people like you and me. They drive themselves to work; they pick up diapers or fast food on the way home; they watch television at night just like you and me. None of these people had anything handed to them, and they're not going to be featured on the front of *Fortune Magazine*. They didn't go to Ivy League schools. These are everyday people we can relate to who all had to start from scratch in the corporate world.

What's remarkable about these people is that they found the secret to security and benefitted financially—something that we can all learn from and stand to do better. This is a group of people who sleep well at night. The key is they wrangled control away from employers and placed it their own hands; they brought the control back to their side of the table. And the good news is that their strategy of bringing control back to their side of the table—and out of their employers' hands—is a strategy that can be copied.

Worry Less

The first thing that the people in this book did was reverse the worry cycle. They bit the bullet and went out on a limb in their careers—in little ways and in big ways. Gradually, as they took more responsibility, they started earning more money. As they made more money, their confidence grew; as their confidence grew, they took more responsibility and gradually made even more money. That's the kind of cycle we all want to enact in our own lives.

So instead of complaining about your stagnant income, you can learn another way from the folks in this book. They can help inspire you to get out of the worry cycle and get into a success cycle where you see your income and confidence grow. If we're able to implement some of these simple worry-less tips that we talk about throughout the book, then we're more likely to be productive business people. Instead of always looking over our shoulder, we're able to look forward and be productive.

HUNT

My first book was about people who were fed up with corporate jobs and started their own companies. I described their entrepreneurial mindset with the acronym HUNT: H, Harness what you have; U, Underestimate obstacles; N, Notice your network; and T, Take the next step. We admire entrepreneurs because the vast majority of us want to start our own business. But what that really means is, we want the control over our own lives that a business *seemingly* gives us. The harsh reality is that most people will never take this step. More than half of business owners (I don't subscribe to research that says 95 percent of small businesses fail) decide their business is too much to handle and go back to working a job.

Happy Medium

Of course, there's always the headline entrepreneurs who show up in the local business chronicle as success stories—and that's fantastic. You can find a few hundred of these people each year in the average metropolitan area. For my first book, I met with dozens of entrepreneurs, and they are proud of their success. They've made it through the obstacle course. But for every person who has been successful, there are ten people who wish they could make that leap— but at the end of the day, they just can't do it. That's the reality of

America. The long-term benefit of starting your own company is you have a tangible asset to sell. Building and then exiting a business may take years of toil. Many people find that instead of starting their own businesses, it's worth it for them to find a happy medium: using an entrepreneurial mindset even if they're in a corporate environment.

The very thing that made these entrepreneurs successful—their entrepreneurial mindset—can be practiced at our jobs. We can learn to think and act with an attitude of ownership over our careers at any size company—large or small—so that we take back the control. Control equals freedom, and freedom equals choice. When you feel like you have choices—instead of letting your employer call the shots— you can live a life with less worry. The HUNT methodologies can apply to your corporate job as well. This book is full of examples from people whose stories are proof that the entrepreneurial mindset can help you find security and independence while still working for some- one else. I wrote this book because for every person I meet that has a successful business, I meet ten more people who say they feel like they are entrepreneurs working inside of a company. That second group has found the middle ground by leveraging their employer's resources.

The people in this book share the stories of how they took owner- ship of their careers, how they grew to feel more in control, earned and asked for a bigger slice of the pie, and ultimately built wealth. They ran their careers as if they were their own companies. That's what made them sleep well at night. And as a financial planner work- ing under the auspices of a large wealth management firm, I feel like I fit in with this group as well.

Best of Both Worlds

Even though I had my own business in college, in the world of finance, it's difficult to start out without a larger organization. Here I was, barely drinking age, expecting people to trust me with their money. I realized I needed some kind of big company to add credibility, so I interviewed with all the big investment firms looking for a career in financial planning. Ultimately, I picked a company that I had some familiarity with—the one my uncle worked for. He said, "If you're going to go to one of these firms, you might as well come here. I can tell you these are good people." My uncle also told me something else—that I was on my own and there was no talk of a partnership with him. I had to go out and find my own clients, but at least I had the credibility of a well-known investment firm on my business cards, a nice cubicle, and some great teachers. Over the years, I've found the best of both worlds.

No matter where you are in your career and regardless of your financial health, you can find more control over your job and add to your sense of security. One of the important things is to avoid living paycheck to paycheck with no cushion—which is how most Americans live. This is the root of all stagnation. If you're truly living paycheck to paycheck and in debt, it's difficult to take any career risks. If you're in that position, work at being your own cushion. In Chapter 4, "Sell from the Heart," you'll meet Buddy Newell, who got through his hard times by working a couple jobs and a huge amount of hours; in the end, though, he found a career that provided financial security. It may take time, but everyone can find more financial and career security.

The key is the entrepreneurial mindset; it's the road to the best of both worlds. The entrepreneurial mindset is one of leadership, ambition, and drive—it works when you have your own company, and it works when you're an employee within someone else's company. The entrepreneurial mindset is like the law of gravity: It works wherever you are—whether you have your own business or a job. The entrepreneurial mindset works wherever you go.

The more of these qualities you have, the more your company will look at you as a partner than just an employee, which is the key to freedom and earning power.

Partner with Your Employer

Following is a checklist of qualities that define a person who has ownership of his or her career. See how many you can check off; it doesn't matter if you possess some or all of these qualities right now, reading this book can help you improve your situation, whatever it may be.

- **Do you get a share in the profits?** A profit-sharing plan means the company puts a percent of profits into your plan account, tax deferred, every year that it's profitable.

- **Do you have a stock purchase plan? Is it favorable to employees?** Many publicly traded companies will let you put up to 30 percent of your salary into company stock; you get to buy at a discount, and they match it with stock options.

- **Are you eligible for performance bonuses?** Companies can give you quantifiable goals to receive bonuses. Even if you're not in sales, if you reach a goal by a certain date, you and your whole department get a cash bonus.

- **Do you get 401(k) matching?** Look for the standard. Companies routinely give at least 50 percent of up to the first 6 percent of your salary deferral.

- **Is your performance measured and reviewed?** Ask for a schedule of regular quarterly reviews to monitor your progress toward a promotion or raise.

Not All Sales Careers Are Created Equal

Here are some things to look for in a sales career:

- A sales quota that does not reset to zero every single year.

- A commission that renews on the retention of clients.

- An opportunity to run a sales team and get credit from those working beneath you.

- A reasonable percentage commission on sales.

- A history of consistency with your cut of the deal; in other words, commission rates don't change from year to year (unless they go up!).

If your employer doesn't offer some of these incentives, don't despair. Many companies are open to negotiating incentive pay to keep their valuable employees happy.

Part I
Harness What You Have

The first principle of the HUNT, the *H*, is about harnessing your drive and talents. When you do what you're innately good at, it's easier to feel connected to work, take ownership of your careers, and reverse the worry cycle. If you started your own business, you would find your drive in the love you have for your product or service—but this book isn't about loving the software you invented and built a business around or loving handmade Italian shoes so much that you open your own shoe boutique. This book is about finding a job—or tweaking your current job—so you feel energized and connected to your work. Even though this emotional connection is crucial to your success at work, it's very rare. Most people are tuned out at work. Only about 26 percent of the workforce is engaged in their jobs, according to a Gallup study.[1] The way to beat the statistics and stay engaged is to find an emotional connection to your job—you may not necessarily love every day-to-day detail, but you need to at least love what the benefit is to the people who use your company's product or service—or the benefit it provides to your career.

If you don't love what your company is doing for your career or what it does for its customers, this book can help. These pages are filled with stories of people who had to make changes in order to find the sweet spot, where they found enthusiasm and love for their jobs. Some of the stories in this part of the book are about regular people

[1] *Fast Company*, Issue 49, July 2001, page 88, "Marcus Buckingham Thinks Your Boss Has an Attitude Problem."

who weren't in the right careers and had to switch, even at a mature age. Others found a good career fit early on. Either way, these stories highlight the value of harnessing what you have and using it at a company you can believe in. If you think your company's product is a rip-off or you have no chance to ever excel, you might as well go home because you'll get eaten up from the inside out. You owe it to yourself to make the needed changes, and these stories can show you how.

Compartmentalize

As you make changes and take on projects that harness your talents, you might find that worry kicks in and paralyzes you. For instance, when I started my radio show—the first call-in radio show I'd ever done—I was nervous throughout the entire week until I would have a chance to fully prepare. Usually my preparation time didn't happen until Saturday (the day before the show), so my entire week was compromised with this underlying feeling of anxiety. Now that I realize it takes me 5 solid hours to prepare, I can stop worrying about the preparation time. I "compartmentalize the project" by scheduling two different 2½ hour planning blocks during the week; my anxiety evaporates as long as I make sure to use those planning times. So compartmentalize your efforts at making changes. Make sure you have some time each week—or each day—to put time and energy into making changes. You're doing it already; you're taking the time now to read this book.

Natural Edge

First you need to find your natural edge. One of the best ways to do that is to read about people who found their edge. Everyone in this book found their edge, but the stories in Part I are especially striking. Linda Rabb has an edge for selling, but she didn't realize it until someone else told her so. Ralph Olson is great at strategy and honed that skill with the help of a mentor early in his career. Bill Reihl has a knack for setting and attaining goals, which he discovered at one of his first teen jobs managing a boat dock. Buddy Newell loves to help people live in the moment by finding immediate gratification, and it took a marriage counselor to help him figure that out. Jennifer Allyn is great at rallying people around a cause. All of us have an edge.

What's your edge? As you read this book, ask yourself that question. If you sincerely don't know the answer, ask other people what they think you're great at. You'll find clues to your edge in your hobbies or your vivid memories of being excited about something you did at your first job. You can figure out your edge—or maybe you already have.

Once you know your natural edge, you need to find the right industry and company to use that edge. If you're miserable at work right now or are not advancing, it could be that you're in the wrong industry or just the wrong company. No one enjoys the work of finding another job, but the stories in this book can help energize you if that's what you need to do.

Value Log

Whether you think you're in the right job or not, it's always important to keep track of your successes. That's how you'll know whether you've found your natural edge: You're succeeding at tasks. If you don't feel like you have a very long list, talk it out with a trusted friend. Many people hold themselves back from success because they don't recognize their contributions at work. So make that list—and keep adding to it. Every day you do something that adds value to your company, so make sure you're keeping track.

There are two reasons to keep track of the value you add to your employer. For one thing, your success will fuel your enthusiasm. For another thing, you have to think of yourself as a free agent nowadays; we have to be on our toes because, for better or worse, today's workplace is ever-changing. If you have a value log, you'll sleep better at night knowing you have this portfolio of value that could be transferred to another job or even to another industry. Keeping a value log ensures you'll have a contingency plan if your job disappears in a corporate merger. Remember: It's not just *what* you do but what people *know* you do.

Learning

Another important part of harnessing what you have is to continue to learn—and reading this book is one way to learn. What I want you to learn from this book is that you can *be yourself* even when you work for someone else. One of the first assumptions most of us have is that in order to be a "company man" (or woman), we need to change ourselves and fit in like a cog in a machine. We try to fit into an organization *too* well. The problem with fitting in too well is that we forget all about what we have to offer, what makes us special, and we feel squelched. Of course, we have to pay attention to dress codes and company standards of behavior, but we can still be ourselves. The people who keep their personal integrity and personal edge are the ones who succeed in corporate America. The ones who fit in are a dime a dozen.

Work can also be a great place to learn new things and sharpen the skills you already have. So take a risk and volunteer for projects where you can learn something new. Most people don't like to do this; they become part of the dead wood in the undergrowth. Every time you volunteer to learn something new, you set yourself apart at work as someone who's growing and vibrant, not dead wood. And you become even more valuable to your employer.

Compensation

You need to feel like you're paid what you're worth. If you feel underpaid, there are ways to get the compensation you deserve— either at your current job or at another one. First of all, performance should lead your compensation; your compensation should not lead your performance. We'd all like someone to give us a raise and say, "Okay, maybe that money will help you do something great." Instead, in the real world, we have to do something valuable first. And when we do, that's the time to go to our boss and point out that we have added value to the company and expect to see it reflected in a raise within a reasonable timeframe. If they don't, a competitor will.

Here's an important note on compensation: Look for compensation that builds so that every year you're not starting from zero. In my career, for instance, it's known as "fee-based planning," essentially charging a low annual fee instead of an up-front, one-time commission. In the beginning when I was starting out, it was very difficult to make a living charging a low annual fee; it's much less money than up-front standard commissions. For example, if a financial planner sells a $100,000 variable annuity investment to a client, that planner could potentially receive up to $5,000 in commissions; but that variable annuity may never pay the advisor again. After he sells it, the planner is on longer compensated for advice. However, a fee-based planner may take the $100,000, invest it for client, charge a 1-percent fee paid out over the course of a year, for a total fee of only $1,000. Essentially that's only $250 four times a year. Although that didn't seem like much to me, I realized the power of sacrificing the one-time payment in return for a repeating fee. Eventually, as your client list grows—and their money grows—that 1 percent can become much more substantial. As you grow your client's assets, you also grow your income.

At the same time it works out much better for the client. Instead of being "forgotten" after an initial sale, the relationship reinforces the fact that the client is essentially paying as they go, and the advisor has to consistently prove to be a worthwhile value. This puts the client and the advisor on the same side of the table and can lead to very healthy long-term relationships where both parties benefit. I always thought that it would be frightening to have to start every new year from zero—searching for commissions. The decision to operate my business in this "fee-based" manner has contributed more to the "worry less" part of my life than anything else! Instead of starting from scratch at the beginning of every year, my income builds upon itself!

Ask yourself: "At my current job, is there a way to harness my inherent abilities to create an income stream that compounds upon itself each year?" You'll find out more about this when reading about Linda Rabb in Chapter 1, "The Compound Income Effect."

Even for jobs that don't make commissions, there are performance-based bonuses. Even if your employer doesn't regularly offer them, there's a good chance you could negotiate some kind of performance-based bonus. For instance, tell your boss you'll take on an extra project, and if it's up and running by a certain date you get a bonus. *A special note about bonuses*: They're a way to build real wealth. I know of many people who have retired early because they never spent any of their bonus checks and instead invested them for retirement. Saving up a few hundred dollars every month is certainly important, but if you can throw a few thousand dollars into your savings once a year in bonus money, you'll start to sleep very well at night!

Success Stacking

Stack your successes and don't start from scratch every year. Just as an entrepreneur builds his business every year, your responsibilities should build on themselves. If you manage a team of five now, then you want to manage a larger team next year. If you're in charge of one process in logistics this year, you want to work toward being in charge of several parts of logistics next year.

Many career books talk about how to climb the corporate ladder, but I say forget about that. You're in charge of this effort; you're not sitting around expecting the advancements to come to you if you can just find the right way to compliment your boss's tie. Instead of climbing the corporate ladder, you're building your own ladder within the company—or maybe in another company. You can build your own ladder to success.

Here's a list of the hallmarks of a career where you harness what you have:

- You love the benefit your company's product or service provides to customers and to yourself.
- You give yourself credit and keep a written list of your accomplishments.
- You're constantly learning.
- You're properly compensated and have negotiated some sort of incentive-based pay. You feel like you're getting paid what you're worth and are in the position to harness your abilities to create more income!
- You stack your successes. This allows you to build your own corporate ladder to success.

Wes's Worry Less Tips

► **Write it down.**

At the beginning of each year sit down and write out the year's goals—both business and personal. I started doing this early in my career because worry was consuming me: At age 24, my hair was falling out in clumps, and I'd even resorted to hair-growing medication to stem the loss of hair. Now that I figured out that writing down a year's worth of goals helps me mentally chill out, I haven't lost a hair since.

► **Turn roadblocks into resources.**

Figure out a way to turn bad things into good ones. I regularly face 45 minutes of slow traffic during my morning drive to work. Instead of complaining and worrying about how much time I was losing, I started using those times to record interviews for my last two books. Probably 45 percent of my interviews for this book and my last one were done while sitting in Atlanta traffic. I used to hate traffic—now I love it.

For more Worry Less Tips, visit www.wesmoss.com.

1

The Compound Income Effect

—Linda Rabb (from Steak n Shake to Aflac)

Hard work alone didn't get Linda Rabb to her six-figure salary. In fact, she worked hard all her life but never got rich at the work she did in the fast-food industry. Only after making a change—finding a way to compound her income instead of just drawing a paycheck—did Linda turn her hard work into a six-figure income. Now, after only 5 years of selling supplemental insurance for Aflac, the "Steak n Shake Lady" makes well north of $150,000. What's more, she expects to reach a point where, *without working forever,* she can make money each year virtually as long as she lives. I'll explain that part later in the chapter.

Linda didn't always have such high expectations: Most of her life she had worked hard in the food and beverage industry and was happy to just get by. Her last job, as a beverage manager, was okay. But no matter how hard she worked, she still earned the same amount: "It didn't matter how good a job I did, I was only going to be paid X amount of dollars a year," Linda recalls. This started to bother Linda when she reached her 50s. That's when a sudden out-of-state relocation to be near her daughter resulted in Linda working one of the hardest jobs of her life: night manager at a Steak n Shake restaurant. It was what she called a "job of necessity," not a dream career. In fact, most of her coworkers were there because they needed money: "People there are not in it for the laughs and giggles," she says. But it was the best job she could find in a new state with no contacts. For 3 years she worked the night shift 60 to 70 hours a week on a hard concrete floor, earning $42,000 a year.

When Linda talks about how she was working hard and not getting ahead, she has a sense of humor about it. But it must have been an awful feeling for this smartly dressed grandmother-to-be slaving away for what she now thinks of as pocket change. She didn't know what she was going to do, but she knew she had to come up with a plan. So Linda was ready to listen when one of the Steak n Shake regular customers made her an offer: "This gentleman kept coming in and saying if I ever wanted a career instead of a job, I should come talk to him." So Linda went to talk with the Aflac regional sales coordinator. "I knew within 15 or 20 minutes I could do this."

The Triple Rs

Years of working in hourly and salaried jobs had taught Linda an important lesson that is the point of this whole book: She did *not* just need a paycheck; instead, she needed repeatable, reoccurring revenue. For years she'd been trading her hard work for a paycheck, and it hadn't gotten her very far. With Aflac, she'd found a company that offered the ability to set up what I call the Triple Rs: repeatable, reoccurring revenue.

First, she has to land an account (by convincing a business manager to adopt the plan on Aflac's menu of insurance offerings). Then she presents the coverage and hopefully signs up some employees to buy it. That's how she earns her first R: *revenue*, in the form of commissions. The second R, *repeatable*, then comes from sales through word of mouth. Sometime during the first year, at least one of the employees who signs on is likely to use his or her benefits—maybe the employee breaks his wrist or throws out his back. Bam, he gets a check from Aflac. He tells his coworkers about it, and the next time Linda goes to make her presentation at that company, more employees are likely to sign up—with no extra effort on her part. She's selling the same product and making the same number of presentations, so each year her commission base (revenue) grows and compounds. That's what makes her commission income repeatable. Now here's the third R: Aflac also gives Linda *reoccurring* income because each time one of her customers renews his or her policy, Linda gets a commission check. Same customer, new sale each year. What's more, Aflac is able to produce statistics to show that after a customer renews coverage, he or she is extremely likely to keep renewing the Aflac coverage indefinitely. The beauty of the three Rs is that Linda's personal income can now compound instead of having to be replaced every year.

Here's the kicker: After Linda is an Aflac agent for 10 years, whether she continues to work for Aflac or not, she's *vested for life* in those reoccurring commissions. What a great bonus for her retirement years.

Starting from Scratch

Linda had done sales once before, selling cosmetics through multilevel marketing. We've all heard of these kinds of companies where you give home parties, give your sales pitch, and hopefully sell some products. But what Linda found—and so many people have this experience—was that she would have to use her profits to buy more inventory to keep doing more presentations. Even when she was the number-one seller in her area of Arkansas, it never seemed like she could get ahead selling cosmetics.

But Linda saw that selling for Aflac would be different because she wasn't making a one-time sale and hoping the customers would come back when their lipstick ran out. Instead, she would be selling an important product to a growing group of people who would likely renew their coverage, plus she had few up-front costs: "I could become my own business owner for about $300," Linda said. "They put everything I needed to do my business right on my doorstep, postage paid." All she had to do was secure her state insurance license, abide by corporate policies, and work hard.

In the beginning, this was a typical week: Up at 7 a.m., out the door at 8 a.m. and sell Aflac; at 2:30 p.m., arrive at Steak n Shake, change into her uniform in the restroom, and work until midnight; from 1 a.m. to 7 a.m., sleep, and then get up and start all over. Her 2 days off from Steak n Shake—Wednesdays and Thursdays—she would sell Aflac all day long. "There was no time off."

After 3 months of this, Linda realized that instead of giving her financial security, earning the paycheck from Steak n Shake was taking valuable time away from selling the lucrative Aflac products. "Every day I stay on that job being paid a salary, I am losing money," Linda recalls. "I am never going to succeed at this unless I give it 150 percent."

Underestimating Obstacles

Linda remembers that she had only $456 in the bank when she decided to quit Steak n Shake. To her, she was already ahead: monthly rent was only $350, and that left $100 for gas. There was enough food in her pantry, so she figured she would have something to eat. That's what I call confidence. "When I decide to do something, I don't let anything stand in my way," Linda says.

She needed that confidence because one of the drawbacks of selling for Aflac is that it's straight commission. That's right, no paycheck. Even though the company gives its sales associates training and marketing materials—and a huge marketing campaign based on the Aflac duck—it doesn't give you a paycheck. For a lot of people, that might be too much of a drawback. But for someone in Linda's position—she had few household expenses and was willing to work long hours to get started—forgoing a paycheck and living off commissions was a smart decision.

There was another major roadblock that Linda turned into a plus: lack of contacts. Instead of starting out with a list of leads from former coworkers, family, and the usual contacts we all have in our communities, Linda was starting out with nothing. Remember, she'd moved to be near her daughter and spent all of her time working at Steak n Shake. Basically, she had no business or community contacts. That could be a huge stumbling block for a beginning salesperson, but Linda made it her strength. Not knowing anyone made her work harder: "I didn't know anybody, so I knocked on more doors than anybody else."

Also Linda believes in Aflac's insurance products, which makes it easy for her to believe that she can make a living off of selling them. Early on, she saw how the insurance saved a customer of hers: a single mother who was later diagnosed with cancer. When the woman returned to work, she actually ran up to Linda and hugged her because she was so grateful she'd bought the insurance. "I have seen these policies save people's homes," Linda says.

Building Momentum—Simply

Linda built on a selling philosophy that she calls "Keep it simple." She tells people what they're buying, what coverage it gets them, and how much it costs. "That's all I want to know when I go buy a car," Linda reasons, so that's how she presents it. Basically, Aflac is supplemental insurance that pays out a set amount for accidents, cancer, and sometimes even preventive care—such as mammograms. Generally, employers don't pay for the care, but they allow Aflac representatives to come in and talk to employees to let them choose whether they want to have a payroll deduction to pay for the policy. Because Linda might only get a few chances a year to make her presentations to a company's employees, she rehearses her sales speeches to make sure they're easy to understand.

It paid off because Linda landed some accounts from some pretty casual conversations with people she met while she was out and about. She once got an account from a woman she met at a gas station. Linda was pumping her gas and saw a woman trip and fall down. The woman was hurt badly enough that she couldn't drive herself to the hospital, so she and Linda sat on the curb waiting for the ambulance. When the woman—who mentioned she didn't have health insurance—asked what Linda did for a living, she told her about Aflac. When the woman found out the insurance would pay a fixed amount out for accidents and injuries, she said, "You mean they would have paid me for this sprained knee?"

Of course, Linda went and talked to the owner of the small manufacturing company where the woman worked. She arranged a meeting with him and did her "keep it simple" presentation, which convinced him to adopt Aflac as an offering for his employees. And with the injured, uninsured coworker's sprained knee fresh in their minds, the employees adopted it eagerly. That's why, no matter what situation she finds herself in, Linda has a ready speech about Aflac's products. At a moment's notice, she can explain insurance, a topic that makes most people's eyes glaze over when you mention it. But Linda's enthusiasm and belief in the product and general friendliness give her a natural ability to approach people about buying insurance. "You don't get anything that you don't ask for," she says. "If you want to receive, you've got to ask."

Linda learned to think outside the box—so that her customers might do the same. No matter how many times she met with employers who said, "No, my employees can't afford that," or "My company doesn't need that," she let it roll off her back. She approached each meeting with an employer fresh, as if all the other "no"s hadn't happened because she never knew which meeting would be successful.

One early success was when she approached a homebuilder, expecting to set up a meeting with his employees to maybe sell a few policies. Instead, the owner, who couldn't afford health insurance for his employees, started asking a lot of questions. "He kept asking me about different products, and I kept going to the car to get more," Linda remembers. When he saw the relatively low price of the Aflac premiums—which normally are paid by the employees themselves— he ended up buying the supplemental accident insurance for all his 40 employees himself. And as his business grew and he added employees, he bought more coverage.

In her first full year with Aflac, Linda earned $35,000, and in year two doubled it to $70,000. Then in her third year—even when she was laid up for 4 months with back surgery—Linda still managed to sell $352,000 in annual premiums and earn $140,000 for 8 months of work. Pretty amazing at age 57, especially considering that fewer than 3 years before she had been making less than a third of that managing a Steak n Shake!

Taking the Next Leap

If Linda's job were only about making a sale, she probably wouldn't be as successful as she is. Luckily, not only is she good at selling, but she keeps her hard work ethic and makes it her priority to keep her customers happy. "My job only begins when I sell a policy," she says. "I have a responsibility to that client." So as her business started to grow, Linda hired an assistant to work out of an office and answer customer questions and manage paperwork. The assistant works for Linda and is paid out of her commissions. "My business could not grow anymore as long as I kept that small mindset."

After a year selling for Aflac, Linda got her foot in the door at a hospital with 7,000 employees. It was a huge opportunity, and she made the most of it. She sold $100,000 in annual premiums in the

first year, while the four other Aflac enrollers sold only a total of
$75,000 between them. The second year she sold $200,000 to the
hospital's employees, and she still manages that account today.

Her secret, she says, is to be an early riser and "do not procrasti-
nate." When she counsels new sales associates, Linda tells them the
following: "If you think this is the right thing to do, have enough faith
in yourself that you step up and do it. So what if it doesn't work the
first time. Get up and do it again. A baby fails the first time he tries to
walk. What are you going to do? Say, 'that's it, kid, you don't get
another chance?'"

In 2005, Linda moved up to district sales coordinator, where she
still sells and services her existing accounts but also hires and trains
new Aflac associates. Now she has ten active people working below
her, and she gets a portion of sales of each associate in her district—in
addition to the commissions on her own sales.

Now, at age 62, Linda has no financial worries. In just 5 years she
went from being totally unversed about the insurance industry to
making it her lifeblood. Everywhere she goes, Linda wears a crystal
duck broach as a symbol of the Aflac Corp. "I get comments on that
duck," Linda says. It starts conversations in line at fast-food restaurants, helps her sell, and also gives her a constant reminder of her
lucrative career—built on hard work and the power of compound
income.

Wes's Worry Less Tip

► Enough is enough!

We work hard on our careers, and we sometimes worry whether we've made mistakes or done something totally wrong. It's hard to know when to let go and just wait for the results. Linda learned that worrying about results can become crippling. Bringing up her three children, she was always worried about whether she was doing enough to set them on the right track. For the longest time she was worried what would happen to them and realized she had to let them go and let them be adults; they needed to be people who would make great decisions as well as their share of mistakes. This attitude also helps her in business; she puts her best efforts forward, but she doesn't expect all her efforts to totally pay off perfectly. We would all worry less if we realized there's no such thing as a nicely paved road in business—it's always an obstacle course. If you worry, you are defeated before you walk out the door. In business we have to do our best presentations, try our best to sell our new idea or get new customers…then, we have to wait and let our efforts bear fruit.

"…after you have done all you can do—Stand"

—from St. Paul's letter to the Ephesians 6:14

For more Worry Less Tips, visit www.wesmoss.com.

2

Embrace Risk

—Ralph Olson (Pepsi, E-Z-Go Golf Carts,
Gibson Greeting Cards, and R.A. Jones)

Ralph Olson only knows one direction—moving forward—no matter what obstacle or risk might stand in his way. He grew up having to face the world head on growing up in gang-ridden, downtown Philadelphia. Still, he was determined to succeed in the face of risk, so he went head to head with his parents and even his football coach, Joe Paterno. Later, in the business world he faced the challenges of Harvard elites, Fortune 100 companies, and his wife's cancer diagnosis—head on. His determination earned him an amazing career and may have even saved a life.

Early in his business career, Ralph observed that not everyone took to risk as well as he did, especially the "bluebloods" with Harvard pedigrees. "I was raised with adversity at every step," Ralph says. "So when adversity would come to call, the bluebloods had difficulty dealing with it, but I could respond to it in a calmer, more realistic, objective way. My approach was, if you don't want it, then I'll take it."

In the business world, adversity comes in the form of difficult projects, the ones that no one wants because the projects are likely to fail—and that can be a career breaker. No one wants to be in charge of a project that fails. But Ralph was willing to take the risk of any sizably challenging project; in fact, he seemed to thrive on it. He figured it was his edge, and he used it to outshine those with more elite Ivy

League pedigrees. The first remarkable project that launched Ralph's career was the challenge of the world's first 2-liter plastic bottle. I'll refer to it as the "plastic bottle project."

Back when he was a financial analyst at Pepsi Cola, Ralph was offered a project that others turned down: bring to market a plastic soft drink container that would be attractive to consumers and cost-effective to manufacture. "They were looking for somebody to grab hold of the technical side of the process and make business sense out of the whole thing," Ralph says. "I saw it as a tremendous opportunity. Yeah, I could do this. My thinking was 'I want it because I think I can make it work.'" He did make it work, and now the 2-liter plastic bot-tle is part of our culture; people even make bird feeders out of the things. It's hard to imagine this was considered a risk, but that's Ralph's point: Most problems are surmountable, if only we can find the courage to face them.

"When you are challenged with a risky situation," Ralph says, "go forward and close the door behind you." Don't leave yourself a way to back out of the situation. On every project Ralph tackled, he did just that—he closed the door behind him. And the first door he had to close was with his parents and their attitude toward his college education.

Starting from Scratch

There once was a time when children were expected to literally pay back their parents for raising them: half of their paychecks for the first 5 years of work would go back to their parents. Ralph's parents, who were first- and second-generation Americans, expected this of him, just as their parents had expected it. So when Ralph told his par-ents he was going to college first, he was taking the risk of going against tradition and enduring their anger. Still, Ralph stood firm and said he would go to college—on his own dime—and then pay them back a certain amount based on what they thought he would earn those first 5 years after college. In his working-class Philadelphia neighborhood in the 1950s, his parents didn't come off sounding as unreasonable as they do now.

So Ralph rebelled and went to college at Penn State because he had a chance to walk on to its Division I football program. This was another risk because neighboring Villanova University (with a less prestigious D-I program) was offering him a guaranteed full scholarship. Luckily, Ralph performed well at his Penn State tryouts and earned a spot on the team, as well as a full ride for tuition, room, and board. In addition to football, he had to work whatever part-time job he could find to pay for extras such as clothing. He'd defied his parents, so going back to mom and dad for help was not an option.

Enter Joe Paterno, the legendary Penn State football coach, who showed Ralph the importance of teamwork and showed him he could push himself to achieve more than he ever thought he could. One day, Paterno had Ralph over to his house for a home-cooked meal and told him to start thinking about his career because he wasn't going to the pros and may actually play less in his senior year than he did as a freshman. Ralph argued and protested—at first—but then realized Paterno's judgment was right. That's when he threw himself into his engineering studies and started thinking of a business career. His goal: to wear a white shirt.

Ralph's career goal came from an experience he had as a 12-year-old, when he started caddying at a country club. "I saw a whole world that I'd never seen before," recalls Ralph, whose father was a factory worker. "I had no idea what these people did for a living, but I wanted to be one of them." And, he noticed, they all wore white shirts, while his father and all the neighborhood men wore blue shirts to work. Ralph was going to have a white-collar job.

Graduating with a mechanical engineering degree from Penn State, Ralph took a job offer from Crown Cork & Seal, which manufactured beverage containers for the soft drink industry. Immediately, he saw that an advanced degree was necessary; engineering salaries tended to have a ceiling that was reached after only a few years. At first he considered a master's degree in engineering but then realized that ultimately he would be better off long-term to study business and management—he wanted to be a vice president by age 40 and president by age 50. So he enrolled in an MBA program in night school at the University of Pennsylvania's Wharton School of Business. It was a hectic period, with Ralph working by day and studying at night.

First, he had to pay back his parents—and luckily they had underestimated his starting salary, so he was able to pay them back in fewer than 5 years. Then, because he had little time for socializing, Ralph started spending weekends at the ski slopes, where he combined work and fun as a ski instructor. That was also where he met Ginny, one of the few female ski instructors, who would later become his wife. When his MBA was finished, Ralph started looking to open some more doors.

Underestimating Obstacles

Around graduation time, recruiter companies came in to make their hires from the graduating class at Wharton. Pepsi was on the recruiting list, and someone made the comment that Ralph shouldn't even expect to be interviewed because he was a night-school student. But Ralph, who was used to that kind of ribbing, took the risk of rejection and signed up for an interview anyway. During the interview, he was asked what kind of starting salary he wanted, and Ralph named a figure that he thought was good. Later, when Pepsi's job offer came, Ralph was amazed that the salary was $5,000 more than he'd asked for. He and Ginny were puzzled over this. When he asked Pepsi about it, he was told the higher salary was because they expected Crown, his current employer, to counter. Ralph had a lot to learn about compensation and the business world, and there would be more lessons to come.

Another challenge came from the class of new hires he was working with at Pepsi; they all had Ivy League pedigrees, and introductions always included mentions of where they had gone to school. "Hi, I'm Bill—Harvard. This is Jack—Yale, and Sue from Dartmouth." Ralph, with his undergrad degree from Penn State and MBA from Warton's night-school program, was teased about his background. "This is Ralph. He went to some large agricultural school in Pennsylvania and Wharton for his MBA, but it was the night-school program." Ralph says, "I had to have the confidence to say 'I'm going to neutralize their advantage by working harder, being more determined, not giving up.'" So he came up with his lifelong strategy of being willing to take risks that others wouldn't. Where others saw obstacles, Ralph saw opportunity.

That attitude got him promoted at Pepsi from engineering manager to financial analyst—and he was "fast tracked." Instead of resting on his achievements, he took the major risk of his career so far and tackled the "plastic bottle" problem. Brainstorming with a plastics company's engineering think tank, Ralph saw that the main obstacle was that the engineers weren't thinking about what was economically feasible; they wanted to design spherical bottles that would be a nightmare to stock on shelves. After crunching numbers from Pepsi's marketing department, Ralph urged the engineers to come up with a large conventional-looking container; it would be easier to stock, and the bigger size would boost consumption to offset manufacturing costs. And he also did something daring: He proposed—and got—a 5-year exclusive contract with the plastics company for whatever container they ended up agreeing on. So Pepsi ended up with 5 years of exclusive rights to the 2-liter plastic bottle, which gave the company a huge competitive advantage.

Ralph didn't just solve the bottle problem, he was put in charge of the whole plastic bottle distribution division at age 30. That was when he was given a mentor, Warren Junker, an older executive who was putting off retirement. Junker poured all his time into Ralph, even accompanying him to meetings, and gave him play-by-play analyses of his performance and suggestions about how to improve. It was an amazing experience, which shows the huge importance of finding a mentor.

Junker had sage advice and taught Ralph time management, strategy, and the science of compensation. Ralph learned to reduce chitchat on telephone calls and think through all the possible outcomes before getting into negotiations. Ralph also protested that he made less money than some of the people he supervised. Junker's advice: "Responsibility and action come before monetary rewards. Don't worry, the company will see your good work, and you will be compensated soon enough." After 2 years taking Junker's advice, Ralph was voted in as vice president at age 32, making him the youngest vice president in the company's history at the time. He was making great money, but Ralph wanted to go further. Soon Ralph started to get itchy to move up again, this time to the Frito Lay division of PepsiCo, and that's when he listened to Junker's second piece of advice regarding compensation: "If your employer doesn't reward your accomplishments, a competitor will." And that's when Ralph decided to start taking risks with compensation.

Building Momentum—Adventurously

In the early 1980s, Ralph resigned from Pepsi: "They were flabbergasted." He left the comfort of Pepsi—and his spot in the executive gym—to be vice president of operations at a major paint manufacturer's packaging division. It was part of the sweeping changes at the venerable paint company, which was badly in need of fresh ideas. The way Ralph saw it, this risk was a huge opportunity.

"If you're not president in 3 years," the CEO told him, "I hired the wrong person." The title of division president was something Ralph wanted more than ever, so he set out to improve things. Each year for 3 years he won the company's operational award of the year, a $100,000 prize. Then he stunned executives by giving away half to the people who worked for him—something that was unheard of at the company then. "I said, 'We did this as a team. These people work for me. I owe it to them,'" says Ralph, who raised a few eyebrows. But, as always, Ralph risked disapproval and did what made sense to him. The following year, he won again. As the CEO handed him the check, he asked, "Are you giving half this check away?" But by now Ralph didn't have to justify himself. The third year he got the award again; and after dinner at a posh Phoenix resort, the CEO asked Ralph to take a walk with him around the golf course.

The CEO said, "I'm disappointed. You're not president, and it's been 3 years. Maybe I hired the wrong guy. Why haven't you asked for your boss's job?" Ralph answered that it was the CEO's job to propose the promotion. As they walked the entire 18 holes, the CEO quizzed him on what he would do as president of operations. Ralph could have deferred or squirmed out of the conversation, but he faced the risk and poured out his ideas. By the 18th hole, he'd been officially offered the job of division president; but his boss wouldn't talk about compensation yet. "When I said, 'I need to think about that,' he countered, 'Do you want the job or don't you?'" Ralph recalls. That was Friday night; by Monday morning he'd accepted the job and decided on a 50 percent salary increase, stock options, and another $50,000 bonus if he would be able to double the price of his multimillion-dollar operational division and sell it off. This was a substantial pay raise and a nice guaranteed pay package but taught him a hard lesson. Ralph would come to regret that big salary and small bonus.

On the bright side, there were plenty of pluses. Ralph learned key management techniques, such as the difference between a good manager and a good leader. "A manager tells people what to do, then measures how well they do it," he says. "A good leader instills thinking processes so a person can take initiative and solve problems without you being there." Ralph wanted to be a good leader.

To fulfill his vision, Ralph used an extensive network of very intelligent people, including Ram Charan, the renowned business guru. In a memorable all-night session at the Chicago Hilton, Ralph and Charan went over his strategic plan to turn around his division at the paint company. It was a grueling session fueled by coffee and Pepsi delivered by a wide-eyed room service waiter, who peered in at the room littered with flip-charts and papers taped to the walls.

After that, Ralph set out to make drastic improvements. Part of the problem was that aerosols, a huge part of the company's business, had been discontinued when fluorocarbons were banned. So he let go of 30 percent of the company's employees, which was the hardest part for Ralph. "But in this situation, it was a case of business survival," he says. "If the business failed, no one would have a job."

When the paint company was later sold, Ralph saw his glaring mistake. The value of the business was $28 million when he started, and it sold for $50 million 5 years later. "After I turned it around and added more than 20 million dollars in value, I only got $50,000." Ralph says. "I told myself, 'If this ever happens again, I'll do it differently.'"

Taking the Next Leap

Ralph spent the next few years in a series of business turn-arounds—in companies that made various products, from golf carts to greeting cards. He took on troubled companies that many executives didn't want to touch; it was exhilarating and demanding. And it challenged his ethics; for instance, once he was offered a zero-interest home mortgage if he would send all of the employees of his business to use the same local bank. Ralph chose the ethical decision and refused, not wanting to "owe" anyone anything. Then he found a great company in need of serious turnaround work: R.A. Jones, a packaging industry leader.

While the packaging company had a lot going for it, Ralph decided, the big problem was management. When customers asked for innovative new packaging, management would turn them down and send them to the competitor. By now, Ralph was well acquainted with executives who feared risks, and he was just the person to take them on. But it was a touchy situation because the company was family owned, and the person calling the shots was a family member. Still, Ralph took the risk and fired the late founder's descendant, a 35-year company veteran who'd been groomed to be CEO. That person retained his board seat, however, and came to appreciate Ralph's business acumen.

By taking on the innovative projects, the packaging company prospered, and so did Ralph. He spent 12 years at the company, taking it through two sales. And because he'd learned his lesson about compensation, he took a lower salary and instead asked for a percentage of the sale price. That strategic thinking and risk taking doubled Ralph's net worth.

Just as Ralph transitioned out of his last year at R.A. Jones, his family was faced with devastating news. His wife Ginny, the mother of his two children and his partner since giving ski lessons back in Pennsylvania, was diagnosed with breast cancer. Ralph tackled it just like he faced every big challenge. First, he thought only about the goal: how his wife could beat this cancer. Second, he assembled a team of physicians who were the best in the field to get his wife through this time. And he didn't let fear rule his decisions. For example, when the first surgeon said they needed to operate within days, Ralph quickly pulled every string he could to get a second opinion from a surgeon renowned in the field.

When something like a cancer diagnosis comes into our lives, it can be devastating to our sense of security. It's tempting to give up and let the doctors handle everything. But Ralph and his wife stayed involved, researching the latest treatments and most skilled surgeons.

His attitude was, "Let's find a way to make this better," Ralph recalls. "I didn't ever feel there was any option but success." Just as he had done all his life, Ralph closed the door on the possibility of failure and focused on the solution. Ralph and his wife did everything possible to ensure she overcame the disease—and she did. More than 2 years later, Ginny is cancer free and healthier than ever!

Ralph's way of overcoming adversity is thrilling because he's full of real-world examples of how important it is to own your career and see risks as opportunities. He's the ultimate illustration of how we can have the best of both worlds, with financial rewards that we normally associate with entrepreneurs who start and sell their own companies. Ralph didn't take the risk of starting his own company, but he took the route of an "entrepreneur undercover," fixing existing companies and then cashing out for his employer. Even if we don't all become turn-around experts, we can all take reasonable risks and embrace the hard-to-solve problems. The bigger rewards, after all, come when we take the bigger risks.

Ten Steps for Embracing Risk Like Ralph

- **Build a "success pyramid"**—Pay attention to all the sides:

  Side one: Your capabilities, accomplishments, and what you have to offer

  Side two: Your personal code of ethics and integrity

  Side three: Leadership skills and strategic planning

  Side four: Attitude, will, perseverance, ambition, and drive

- **Follow your ethics**—Stand by the decision you feel is right—even if it is an unpopular one.

- **Be strategic**—Like Ralph's favorite consultant, Ram Charan, you need to peel back layer after layer of the onion to find the root cause of your business problem. If you haven't found the root problem, peel back another layer.

  Visit www.ram-charan.com for more information on this brilliant consultant.

- **Close the door behind you**—When deciding to move forward on any project or decision, don't give yourself the mental option to go in reverse.

- **Find a diamond in the rough**—Find the underlying opportunity in every challenge you are faced with.

- **Get a bonus plan**—Ask for incentive-based pay whenever you can find it. Bosses want to hear that you are willing to take an incentive-based bonus plan over a big guaranteed salary.

- **Will things to happen**—Ask yourself, "Am I giving up too early?"

- **Seek great mentors**—Ralph believes you will encounter several mentors throughout your career and can learn something unique from each one of them.

- **Set age-based goals**—Imagine where you want to be by your 30s, 40s, 50s, and beyond.

- **Manage your time**—Analyze how you spend your days. Ralph's mentor at Pepsi made him chronicle the day into 5-minute increments. They discovered that Ralph's phone calls were way too long. By cutting out long-winded socialization, Ralph added nearly 6 hours of time to his week. If you're thinking you are taking time away from your business associates, remember that you are adding time you can spend with your family.

Wes's Worry Less Tip

► Mental preparation.

Use your entire day wisely by fitting in some time for strategic planning. On the way to a big business meeting, instead of worrying about other people's news (sports pages, Britney Spears, the next box office hits) try something different. Take your time in the car or plane on the way to a big meeting to think through all the possible situations that could arise in the meeting and think up ways to steer things your way. It's like playing chess with your business meeting. When the meeting comes, you'll be fully prepared for any situation that arrives. Ralph's mentor, Warren Junker once scolded him for reading the newspaper on a flight to a business meeting. He told Ralph to leave the casual reading to later in the day and instead think through the coming meeting: "We make the news during the day and read other people's news after the day is over," Junker told him. As audacious as it may seem to think that you can actually make the news, why not? Go for it. It doesn't matter if you're a salesperson, lawyer, doctor, or financial planner, you can make your own news. You are newsworthy.

"If you would not be forgotten, as soon as you are dead and rotten, either write things worth reading or do things worth the writing."

—Ben Franklin

3

Ambition Addiction

—Bill Reihl (Ogilvy Public Relations Worldwide)

At a young age, Bill Reihl learned something that is the whole point of this book: Whether or not you work for yourself, the drive and leadership of entrepreneurs can be applied to a career in the corporate world. Entrepreneurs are driven by a lot of things, and one of the biggest drives is ambition. And Bill freely admits to having an ambition addiction: "Instead of thinking of being a millionaire, I set achievable goals, enjoy the triumph of reaching them, feed off them, and set new ones."

Classically hip, light-hearted, and adaptable to any occasion, Bill is a fantastic example for this book; he didn't envision starting his own business, but he did dream of extraordinary success. He can even put his finger on the exact moment he got hooked by the ambition to succeed: at a high-school summer job working at a local marina on the Chesapeake Bay. Bill worked hard and got himself promoted to dock master, which meant he managed dock traffic—a job that had him supervising dockhands twice his age. Bill remembers barking out orders such as, "Hey Jimmy, there's a 35-foot sloop coming into dock number four. Put him in slip number 52." Even though it was a lot of responsibility for a teenager, Bill thrived on it. "I was bitten by the bug," he recalls. "I wanted to achieve, I wanted to succeed. I thought, 'I got here on my own, I earned this.' Now I'm addicted to that feeling."

Bill reminds us that we all have goals we have achieved along the way. And it's vital that we remember to use any triumph, even the small ones, to prop up our courage and take on the next hurdle, and the next.

"Great things are done by a series of small things
  brought together."

—Vincent Van Gogh

Rising up from small-town roots to the position of executive vice president at Ogilvy Public Relations took a huge amount of ambition and courage. Public relations is such a competitive field, and PR people are a dime a dozen (very much like my field, financial planning), so it can be difficult to rise into upper management. Bill says he was able to quickly rise through the ranks, sometimes leapfrogging a few steps, thanks to the drive he'd absorbed growing up surrounded by people with an entrepreneurial spirit. His mother, a huge supporting force in his life, has always worked and runs her own occupational therapy practice, his father runs a marina, his uncles have fishing boat fleets, one aunt was president of the local bank, another aunt has her own insurance agency, and his grandfather told stories of running the family farm and other businesses and investments on the side to provide for their large family. They were hard-working, well-respected people who had high goals for themselves and a reputation for success in the small town where the family had lived for generations. And when he moved away to the big city, Bill took with him the ambition to succeed. It goes to show how important it is to believe in yourself and surround yourself with people who are good examples.

"It's not about praise," Bill says. "It's about personal challenge." For instance, Bill says he looks down the road 5 or 10 years to figure out where he wants to be—and how his current job will get him there. But while he fantasizes about where he wants to be, he doesn't forget about the day at hand. "I get an old-fashioned satisfaction of a job well-done and a hard day's work," Bill says.

And no matter how menial it may seem, every job has something to teach. Bill's first job at age 13 was a summer job cleaning up at a gas station. Hanging around the mechanics while he swept the floors, Bill learned things he had no clue about, such as how to change car tires and oil. "From that moment on," he says, "I remember saying, 'Each one of the jobs I'm going to have is going to be valuable for me.'"

When it came time to go to college and pick a career, Bill hit the ground running.

Starting from Scratch

First, Bill had to figure out what he was going to succeed at. "I knew I wasn't the smartest guy in the room, or the biggest guy," Bill says. "I was gonna have to win it some other way." As a B-plus, A-minus high-school student, Bill wasn't the valedictorian of his class, but he was class president for all 4 years. So as graduation came around, Bill made some ambitious choices. "I made the brave decision, at the time, to really challenge myself." He would attend an out-of-state private college in Washington, D.C., instead of the in-state Maryland school offering him a full scholarship, and he would work to pay his own way and not burden his parents.

At American University, Bill asked for permission to move into the dorm early so he could "get in the groove of work before school started." He had plenty of part-time jobs—but he always set his sights on better paying jobs than the typical college student jobs, such as waiting tables and painting houses (two of my college jobs). For instance, one of his jobs was as a part-time marketing manager for a real-estate development firm. As always, he found a way to talk to the person doing the hiring, explain his skills, and impress him as someone who could handle the responsibility.

Finally, in his senior year, Bill fit in a full-time job around his class schedule. He would take an early morning class, get out by 8:45 a.m., work all day, then go to another class or two in the evening. The job was as public relations assistant for the American Society for Engineering Education, a professional association that paid him about $18,000. It was a nice little entry-level job because the public affairs person was busy monitoring Congressional committees and let Bill do much of the PR work. Here he was, just 20 years old, and he was sitting in a cubicle writing press releases, talking to journalists, and scrambling to finish schoolwork in his spare moments. "I didn't sleep that much," Bill says. "I was in a fraternity but not very active in it, dated, had friends, and would drive to see family on the weekends. I was always a good schedule manager. I like to work hard and play hard."

As graduation came around, Bill decided to build a PR career. It seemed like a great career where he could fuel his creative side, use his gift of gab, and climb the corporate ladder. Although he had a passing interest in politics, he saw people working in political jobs and didn't like the slow progress. "I saw people work 6 months on something, then it falls apart at the end," Bill says. "I wanted to be in a job where things actually get done! I'm an ambition junkie, and in politics, things weren't moving fast enough." And the place to be for PR, he figured, was New York City: "If you can make it there, you can make it anywhere."

Even though he was a little scared in the back of his mind, on the surface Bill was confident and full of moxie. That's because he'd fueled his ambition with a string of successes throughout high school and college. Whenever he feared the big challenges ahead, he would remember how he'd reached all of his goals in high school and college. So he sat down with the *New York Times* want ads and found an ad for Kahn Communications Group, a small PR firm with an opening for an account executive—a position one step above entry level.

He sent his resume along with a letter explaining that he already had some work experience—and he added, "I'm hungry and ambitious."

Underestimating Obstacles

Human resources people usually weed out job applicants whose resumes don't exactly fit, but Bill's job experience caught the hiring manager's attention, and he got a telephone interview, where he was asked, "Why should I hire you as an account executive?" Bill explained he had plenty of PR work experience already in college—he wasn't the typical inexperienced college graduate. And to follow up, Bill set out with his own direct-mail campaign, sending one or two postcards each week to his interviewer. For instance, one of the postcards showed a black and white photo of President John F. Kennedy and on the back Bill wrote, "Ask not what your country can do for you, ask what I can do for the Kahn Communications Group."

It worked: Bill got an in-person interview in New York City. At the interview, the guy Bill had been hammering with mail had the series of postcards laid out on his desk. The company wanted to hire him, but the problem was they needed someone immediately, and it was March, still 2 months before graduation. Bill sent a follow-up letter with the phrase, "56 days until I can be there," written in huge letters. He got the job.

It was a whirlwind beginning, with plenty of obstacles to overcome—and he overcame each of them in stride. Early Sunday afternoon, after graduation ceremonies, Bill had brunch with his family and roommate, packed up his Honda Civic wagon, and drove to New York City to arrive by nightfall. Monday morning he started his job. That first day he showed up bright eyed, with a mod haircut and a skinny tie. "Some big lumbering guy comes in, throws a press release and media list on my desk and says, 'I hear you're the new hotshot.

Pitch this, get three hits, and come talk to me.'" So Bill started cold-calling journalists, looking to get some executive interviewed by three media outlets. "It was brutal. People curse you out, slam down the phone," Bill recalls. Somehow he got three interviews lined up that day. But, just as he had learned how to fix cars at his first job as a teenager, he was eager to learn more. First, he was going to research and study his client list so he understood the stories in the press releases better; he would learn the deadline days for each of the media outlets; and he would read newspapers and magazines to fig-ure out which stories appealed to which publications. It was a crash course in his new job, but he could learn on his feet.

"I quickly carved out a niche as someone who was willing to take on any challenge," Bill says. "I was a voracious reader; I understood media." That made him good at media relations because he under-stood what each publication wanted. For example, a snarky, sensa-tional story would appeal to the *New York Post*, whereas the more highbrow pitches would go to the *New York Times*.

The biggest challenge was a client nobody wanted: the American Telemarketing Association. "Who wanted to represent the telemar-keters of the country?" Bill says. "At the time, before the national 'do not call' list, telemarketing was at the height of its unpopularity." It was like being a spokesman for assault weapon owners after the Columbine high school tragedy. Those were the days of the Seinfeld episode where Jerry tells a telemarketer he's busy, asks for his home number, and says, "I'll call you back around dinner. I can't do that? Now you know how I feel!" Still, Bill took on the challenge, and at age 24 became chief spokesman for the American Telemarketing Associ-ation. His name appeared on press releases, and he was quoted in major publications. "It was a thrill for me to do that," he recalls.

Shortly after Bill started at Kahn Communications, it was bought out by Ruder Finn, a mid-sized, independent public relations firm headquartered in New York with domestic and international clients.

Suddenly he went from working for a 30-person company with one office to a large company with several hundred people. Bing, another challenge, and Bill was ready, "I was in the groove, really jamming."

Building Momentum—Daringly

After a couple of years, Bill got a call from a mid-sized boutique firm, DeVries Public Relations, which then specialized in fashion, beauty, and lifestyle accounts. "I remember thinking to myself, 'I don't know fashion or beauty, it's not me,'" he recalls. "Then the light goes off in my head: 'a challenge, let's go for it.' So I jumped and went for it."

Moving up to senior account manager wasn't easy at first. For one thing, at DeVries he encountered a boss who was a genius but notoriously difficult and challenging. And for another thing, the clients were bigger and more demanding. But he kept a smile on his face and worked hard every day, adopting the mantra, "Fake it 'til you make it." And, eventually, Bill found a mentor in that same challenging but brilliant boss and made a name for himself. His shining moment was when he was just 26 years old and was given the job of promoting the Fairmont Hotel chain, which was taking over a historic hotel in Boston and restoring it to its former glory. Bill worked hard to set up a PR blitz in Boston for Fairmont Hotel CEO Robert Small. Bill coached Small and had him meet with top editors of nearly every publication in Boston. "I nailed it," he recalls. He got the interviews and "hand held" the CEO, all the while sitting in the presidential suite of the hotel alongside a bunch of 50-year-old guys at the top of their industries. "Here I was 26. I was holding my own," he recalls. "I'm going to celebrate this, enjoy this."

Once again Bill met an ambitious goal. It's almost like he dared himself to achieve things that were supposed to be over his head.

Those years at DeVries were like finishing school for Bill. He went to all the best parties in New York, stocked his closet with tasteful gray suits, and used his gift of gab to network for his clients. And even with all the glitz, he held onto his skill of being able to talk to all kinds of people in any setting. "I can enjoy just about everything," Bill says. "I can go play golf and talk about the stock market, go whitewater rafting, or attend a seminar on Winston Churchill." This works for him in his personal life as well as his professional life. In public relations, every single client has to have an interesting story. "If I have a wide experience, it's easier for me to uncover these nuggets that make a good story."

His wide-ranging experiences also came in handy at DeVries when some clients turned out to be tough customers. In particular, there was a client who would sit down and pound on the table in meetings, which really freaked out some of the PR people, but not Bill: "I just leaned over and said 'We got it. We hear what you're saying.'" Pounding the table for emphasis was just "how they talked," Bill says, as he laughs about the memorable meeting. "They weren't going to hit us!"

With his small-town background and experience in all kinds of life situations, Bill could relate to a lot of different kinds of people—whether it's a CEO, a journalist, or client. Bill says he "could go talk to bankers, lawyers, or acrobats."

Taking the Next Leap

There comes a time when an ambition addict has to stop and take stock. Because, really, there will always be another higher step in one's career—no one ever reaches the top. What's great about Bill is that in his 30s, when he was at the top of his game, he took the chance to slow down and take stock of what *he* wanted, not just what his career demanded. It happened after his next promotion, when he was recruited by BSMG Worldwide, a big multinational company. "I'm being called up to the show now," Bill thought. He would be representing bigger companies with products that were household names, such as Schick razors and Arm & Hammer baking soda. The challenge was to take what he learned promoting cool, high-end companies and apply it to companies that made everyday consumer goods. The time was the prosperous 1990s, when companies had lots of cash to spend on big publicity stunts, and Bill knew how to handle these from his Fairmont Hotels experience.

Yet Bill noticed he was working too hard. "I would push myself, get exhausted," recalls Bill, who learned to take off Sundays, lock himself in his apartment, and "be lazy for a day."

One day, as he took stock of his life, he saw that he wanted something more than New York could offer. "I love New York. It's good to me; it's good for my career," Bill says. "But at 30 years old I was a vice president and still living in a walk-up apartment. I wanted a better quality of life. I wanted more trees, maybe a yard. I told myself, 'You've worked hard. Let's enjoy some of this.' I started to want more than working 15 hours a day."

It was 1999, and Bill's plan was to wind down the year and take some time off to look around the country for a place with a big-city feel but a more laid-back pace. He found the perfect exit strategy in a dot-com, OnlineRetailPartners.com, a company that took brick and mortar retailers online. For 8 months he split his time between the startup and his relocation search. The problem he faced as he talked to different PR firms was that they saw his New York experience and wanted him to work in their New York offices. But he persisted and looked for a job that would keep his New York–level salary and responsibility, and he found it at the Atlanta, Georgia, office of Edelman Public Relations Worldwide.

At Edelman, his main job was to be a link between the Atlanta and New York offices. He stayed on happily for 5 years. Then, in 2005, he found an opportunity to do global PR for big-name brands at the Atlanta office of Ogilvy, a top-ten agency with more than 60 offices worldwide. Finally, Bill thinks he has found a place that can contain his ambition. That's because as executive vice president, he works across disciplines, developing strategy and creativity, handling new business development domestically and internationally, and managing teams in multiple locations. He works with advertising, media buying, promotions, online—you name it—as well as with partner companies across the parent company (WPP) network. "I have a feeling that I can stay in the company and keep my entrepreneurial spirit," he says. "And I can keep climbing up." Who knows, maybe he's the future CEO of Ogilvy. I wouldn't put it past him.

Whatever happens, Bill's ambition is sure to take him to some exciting—and fulfilling—places. His secret is not to be intimidated from pursuing his ambitions. For instance, Bill recently struck up a conversation about art with a big wig in the art museum world. Now, many of us might feel a little worried that we'd say something stupid if we tried to talk shop with someone holding a doctorate in art history. But even though he says his art history knowledge is "about a mile wide and an inch deep," Bill put himself out there and took a risk. "We ended up having a great conversation. I knew just enough to perk up his ears," Bill says. "Now we're talking about representing some major players in the art world." Making new connections like that is all part of the thrill for Bill. When we let our ambitions guide us, the sky is the limit. So sit back and imagine the possibilities. You never know where your ambitions will take you.

Fueling Your Ambition

Even if we're not all as driven as Bill, we can use some of his techniques to give our careers the boost they need:

- Set out to learn something new every single day—whether it's job related or not.

- Talk to everyone you meet about their interests; you'll learn something new and make new connections. Dale Carnegie's *How to Win Friends and Influence People* is recommended reading.

- Before you fall asleep each night, think of where you want to be in 5 years and set small, reachable goals for yourself to get there. Maybe you'll dream of a way to reach your goals that you haven't thought of before.

- Celebrate! Enjoy each accomplishment, whether it's a new job, a new skill (such as standing on your head), or reading an autobiography of someone you admire.

- Articulate your strengths. False humility and modesty don't go very far when you're lobbying for a new job or project. Learn how to talk about your accomplishments without sounding like you're bragging and concentrate on conveying why your skill set will be of value to any organization.

Wes's Worry Less Tip

► Many hands make light work.

It's easy to worry when you're the one coming up with new initiatives at work. We worry that our new ideas may flop, and we're scared to face the consequences. Try this: Before you take a new idea to your boss or client, go get feedback—lots of feedback! It will either confirm the idea is great or help you find holes in the idea before its unveiling. When Bill has a new idea, he talks it over with family and friends, people in elevators and on airplanes, and even the check-out clerk at the grocery store. Take this extra step to ask questions, tease out insights from unexpected places, and see where it takes you. This process will help take the worry out of unveiling a new idea to your boss or a client. Instead of fearing other people's opinions, use them!

"I not only use all of the brains I have, but all I can borrow."

—Woodrow Wilson, 28th President of the United States

Make More, Worry Less Investing*

Once you have the "make more" part of this book down, *then* what do you do with all of that money? Here's something to keep in mind when putting all of your performance bonuses to work. On my financial talk radio show, I refer to it as "Make More, Worry Less Investing."

I've been in the investment business for nearly a decade and have worked with hundreds of families to ensure they meet their retirement and investment goals. My team and I manage more than a quarter of a billion dollars for our clients. I've had the pleasure of working with some fantastic investors—as well as those who continually seem to shoot themselves in the foot. For the purposes of this section, let's refer to the great investors as the "Make more, Worry less" type and the poor investors as the "Worry more, Make less" type.

Here's what happens:

The "Worry More, Make Less" group constantly looks for a better deal, a hotter mutual fund, and listens to what their neighbors are doing with their money. They persistently chase a dream to make more than their peers—and everyone else at the neighborhood cocktail party. I'll get to how this group ends up in a minute...

The "Make More, Worry Less" group looks at their investment career like building a house. They formulate a realistic plan, stick to the plan while building the house, put in a solid four-sided foundation, and enjoy living in the home for years. As major circumstances change, like having children or caring for elderly parents, the house can be modified, updated, or improved upon over the years. This group utilizes the following four steps with their investments:

---

* Remember that this data is historical and past performance is not a guarantee of future results.

1. They formulate a solid financial plan and set realistic long-term expectations for how their money should grow over the years.

2. They set an *asset allocation* plan in place that is in line with their ability to take investment risk and market fluctuation. The asset allocation will determine how much they have invested between stocks, bonds, cash, real estate, and other alternative investment vehicles.

3. They choose the most effective investment vehicle or investment management for each piece of their asset allocation pie.

4. They review the plan four times a year—rebalancing their investments if needed and monitoring for any major changes or shifts that would affect their initial plan.

This process repeats itself from step 1 through step 4 over and over again—and by having each step in place from day one, the "Make More, Worry Less" group historically invests well.

Here's the problem: Most investors fall into the "Worry more, Make less" group and suffer dismal long-term results!

A study[1] conducted in 2006 by DALBAR, Inc., (Quantitative Analysis of Investor Behavior) reveals: From 1986 through 2005, the average annual return for the S&P 500 stock index was 11.9%. In that same period of time, the average annual return for stock investors was a dismal 3.9%. This result barely keeps up with inflation!

What's the culprit? Over that 20 year period, the average stock fund investor held their funds for less than 3 years before switching to another fund! They were constantly chasing funds that had already done well in the PAST! By the time they made the switch, they were always catching the tail end of a trend. How much sense does that make?

---

1. Article published by Putnam Investments that cites the study. Putnam's article is titled "What everyone should understand about investing for retirement." Source cited: DALBAR, Inc., Quantitative Analysis of Investor Behavior, 2006.

Another study[2] managed by professors[3] Brad Barber and Terrance Odean examined 66,000 households and their investment trading habits between 1991 and 1996. The professors discovered that investors who traded the *least* earned more per year—7 percentage points more—then the most frequent traders.

The lesson here is to take the lead from the "Make more, Worry less" group—who formulate a good long-term plan, commit to it long term, and make modifications as needed over time. "Worry Less" doesn't refer to not caring about your money or investments—it just means that constant tinkering, timing, and chasing returns usually turns out badly.

"It never was my thinking that made the big money for me. It was always my sitting. Got that? My sitting tight!"

—Edwin Lefevre (American journalist and writer most noted for his writings on investments and Wall Street business)

For more information on "Make More, Worry Less Investing," visit www.wesmoss.com.

2. *Money Magazine* (September 2007) "The Best Advice of All Time—20 rules for success from some of the smartest investors (and other people) who have ever lived." by Carla Fried

3. Brad M. Barber, Professor of Management, Director, Center for Investor Welfare and Corporate Responsibility Ph.D., University of Chicago. Terrance Odean, Professor of Banking and Finance at the Haas School of Business at the University of California, Berkeley.

4

Sell from the Heart

—Buddy Newell (PK Time and Dubey & Schaldenbrand)

Buddy Newell is a great example of believing in what you do for a living. Oddly enough, it took the stress of a failed marriage for him to look at his career and realize that he shouldn't waste his time in jobs he didn't love. After years of living paycheck to paycheck, Buddy took his hobby—high-end watches—and quickly found a way to turn it into a lucrative career.

It sounds obvious, but many people endure working at jobs that make them miserable—the only reason they go to work is for the money. And guess what? They never make enough money to get ahead. When Buddy talks about his early career, before he found the watch business, he sounds bitter and regretful. Yet when he talks about his years in the watch industry, he beams with happiness. When he took a job for $40,000 a year selling watches, he found a way to make 5 times that within 2 years. That's the power of putting your heart into it.

Starting from Scratch

Buddy's early years were filled with hard work and frustration. First, he went to the University of Miami hoping to earn a business degree. At the time, cocaine distribution was rampant in Miami.

Even at the university, he saw students supporting themselves in the drug business. While he was working for $3 an hour at some little job, these students would come home with suitcases full of cash. When the police raided the dorms one day, they arrested about a quarter of the students on drug charges. "It was like the Wild West. It was crazy," he recalls.

On top of that, Buddy was struggling with the university's policy that required all students to take courses across the curriculum. Buddy balked; he didn't want to study history, he just wanted to take business courses. But the university had its rules, and Buddy was young and impetuous. "Those were frustrating years," he recalls. "I lasted about 2 years in Miami."

He transferred to the University of Maryland, hoping a change in scenery would help. But most universities have the same requirement of taking courses outside your major, and he grew impatient. "I needed it yesterday," he recalls. "I'm not the kind of guy to sit there, read the book, and get an A. I was a real rebel." Eventually he left and moved to New York City, where he had grown up.

He approached a department store manager and said, "Give me a job, all I want to do is work." That's how he ended up working in store security as an undercover detective nabbing shoplifters. When he hurt his back getting tackled while trying to handcuff someone, Buddy quit. "I thought, 'For six bucks an hour putting my life on the line, this is not a good idea.'"

Underestimating Obstacles

Because working for other people wasn't going well, Buddy tried his hand at starting his own business. He had the idea to provide internal security for high-end boutique stores in New York that had problems with employees stealing. Turns out this is a pretty big problem, and he had a good idea. A store would contract with him to pose

as a part-time employee, watching the other employees to see if anyone was up to something. He rooted out some clever scams. Sometimes employees would stash merchandise in a box, pretend it was
trash, and throw it in the dumpster, only to retrieve it later that night.
Another common trick was to ring up an item for $1.99 when it
should have been $199.

"You get to see some interesting things," Buddy says.

Even though he started out enthusiastically, Buddy didn't love his
new venture. And he found out that even though he's a hard worker,
he was overwhelmed with having to run his own business. "I'm very
good at something that's up and running," Buddy says. "But startup
operations, starting from scratch, that's not my forté."

So Buddy was honest with himself and gave up the security business. It's no use trying to fit a round peg in a square hole, and business
startups are not for everyone—which is why I'm writing this book. It's
for people who have an entrepreneurial spirit but want the safety of
working in an existing business.

His next job was as a doorman, and within 3 months he was managing the bellhop staff. "I was working my butt off," he says. The hotel
business was 24 hours a day, 7 days a week. He was excelling at the
job, but he couldn't figure a way to make it meaningful and lucrative.

Finally, to make more money, he worked two full-time jobs: at the
hotel and for his father, who ran a wholesale food supply business.
Buddy was in charge of getting the trucks loaded and out every morning at 4 a.m. and managing relationships with customers. He was good
at this, and the business was successful. "We created a niche in the
market," Buddy says. With real estate leasing for hundreds of dollars
per square foot in Manhattan, restaurants don't have room to store
several days worth of supplies. So daily food deliveries are the norm.

Buddy started some innovations at the business, introducing
healthier food items such as frozen yogurt and bottled water. One of his
successes was to convince a deli franchise to carry bottled water at its
locations. "What, pay money for water?" the deli owner asked. "Who's

going to pay money for water?" Buddy convinced him, and it worked out well. This might have been a great career for Buddy, but problems with his father—who owned the company—made it difficult.

That's when fate took a twist. It was 1993, when the first terrorist plot to bomb the World Trade Center came to light. Buddy was living on 24th Street, pretty close to the buildings, and he knew people who worked there. It shook him up. This was an obstacle he couldn't overcome, so he took up his girlfriend's offer to move in with her in Miami. That move set in motion events that led him to his love.

In Miami for the second time, Buddy did a variety of jobs that didn't amount to anything. He even worked at a temporary labor office, providing security. Many of the laborers were recently out of prison, and when one of the managers was shot and killed by one of the workers, Buddy left. The one bright spot was working at a watch store, selling watches. It was more of a hobby than anything, giving him a discount so he could buy watches for himself.

He'd also gotten married, and that marriage was on the rocks. During a marriage-counseling session, the counselor asked him, "What do you like to do?" And he blurted out, "I'm a watch guy. I enjoy watches." But Buddy didn't see how to take a small-time job selling watches and turn it into a career. The counselor encouraged him: "You'll figure it out." And she was right.

Building Momentum—Enjoyably

Although the marriage wasn't saved, Buddy found his career. At first he worked 100 hours a week just to make enough to support himself. But in the midst of his failed marriage, the job was like a life raft. He truly did enjoy being around the watches and talking to people about them. And not just the watches themselves, but being part of the excitement and pleasure of the purchase. Most of the time a wristwatch is a gift people buy for someone or a reward they buy for themselves. Buddy liked being part of that.

Pretty soon he was giving advice to the owners of the shop: "Never say no to anybody. Once you say no, you've lost that customer." Problem was, the shop often didn't have the ability to customize their watches to what customers wanted. For instance, if a watch had a white dial and the customer wanted a black dial, they would say, "Sorry we don't have black dials." Buddy, however, was all about customer service. He loved making the customer happy and closing the sale. "Let me try and get you the black dial and make you happy" was Buddy's philosophy. He told them, "You know if you don't make that sale, someone else is making that sale." But the shop didn't take his advice.

Buddy had a friend in the watch business from whom he'd bought some very expensive watches. It had been 10 years since he'd talked to the guy, but he knew he sold great merchandise. So if the shop where Buddy worked didn't have the kind of watch someone wanted and wouldn't customize it, Buddy would tell them to call his friend. He would say to people, "Tell him Buddy from Miami told you to call." And they did.

After a while, he called up his old friend and said, "Hey, this is Buddy from Miami, remember me?" The old friend's reply: "Oh my God, you're the one who's been sending me all this business. That's unbelievable." And that's how Buddy found something he could truly put his heart into.

Taking the Next Leap

Buddy started selling watches for his friend on the road through a company that is now called PK Time. Eventually the company wound up being the exclusive representative for Dubey Schaldenbrand watches—an extremely high-end brand of wristwatch made by Cinette Robert, a watchmaker in a small town in Switzerland. These watches cost thousands of dollars.

Buddy understood his customers: They wanted immediate gratification when they came to buy a Dubey Schaldenbrand watch. "The person doesn't want to wait," he says. "Maybe you got a bonus, made some money in the stock market. You want to reward yourself, you want to walk home with the gift tonight, wear it over the weekend." So when customers ask for different watch bands or dials, Buddy finds a way to make it happen.

"I've had phone calls from Las Vegas at 1:00 in the morning from people who just made money in a casino and want to spend it," he says. Once someone called on a Wednesday and wanted a certain $60,000 watch—and he wanted it on his wrist by Saturday. The watch was in Switzerland; the man was in Aruba. Buddy managed to get the watch from Switzerland to Aruba in 48 hours.

With that kind of customer service and loyalty, Buddy worked his way up easily to sales manager and then president of the company.

And he didn't stop there. When customers asked for watches with diamonds on them, Buddy told the designer. Being very traditional, she said she would never make a man's watch with diamonds. When Buddy persuaded her to make just one for his personal use, he sold it off his wrist within 10 minutes of putting it on. That got the watchmaker's attention, and she began taking his suggestions. Customers wanted a Swiss sports watch that could be worn while golfing or swimming—and the watchmaker came out with some. She respected his suggestions so much she even came out with a "Buddy" line of watches. "It was such a special honor for me," Buddy says. "That really made me feel proud."

Even though there are only about 40 other salespeople for that brand in the whole United States, Buddy protected his market even further by being the only one to offer the Buddy designs. And it built credibility with his customers when they saw their requests come out in new designs with Buddy's name on it.

"I love the business. I love what I do," Buddy says.

So it really doesn't make a lot of sense to work in an industry that you don't feel connected to. There is tremendous power in loving what you do. You don't have to really love the product itself—such as insurance or computer software—although it doesn't hurt. What you really have to love is the benefit it provides the people who use it. It could be the instant gratification of a beautiful timepiece or something else that engages you. As long as you love it, you never know where you'll go. Buddy found what he loved, put his heart into it, and found a career beyond his wildest dreams.

Wes's Worry Less Tip

▶ **Revive and thrive.**

When we're worried about our livelihood, sometimes we think working harder will be the solution to our fears. So we put off vacations, eat lunch at our desks, and put our heads down to work harder. But working harder doesn't always mean we work better. We all need time to kick back and relax: Stephen R. Covey calls it taking time to "sharpen the saw" in his *The 7 Habits of Highly Effective People*. Buddy takes worry out of his day by treating himself to a sit in the massage chair in his apartment with an aromatherapy eye cover. Whenever he has to travel for business, he mixes in some relaxation by doing something different—visiting that city's zoo, or taking in a play, or walking through an art museum. Sometimes he just likes to sit near his home on South Beach and people-watch while sipping a Mojito and thinking about what a beautiful beach he lives near. We all have our own little slice of paradise. Take time to revive and then go back to work and see how you thrive with less worry on the brain!

"We must always change, renew, rejuvenate ourselves; otherwise we harden."

—Johann Wolfgang von Goethe

5

Rally for a Cause

—Jennifer Allyn (PricewaterhouseCoopers LLP)

When Jennifer Allyn talks about her career, she gets right to the big questions—such as how to live a good life, how to solve social problems, and how to help make this a better world. Here's the thing about people like Jennifer: They have a huge amount of drive and can achieve amazing things. The drawback: Sometimes people with causes end up working in low-paying jobs at struggling nonprofit agencies. Jennifer's story shows how rallying for a cause can land you in a great job—especially if you rally for your own cause as well as the cause of the greater good. And even if your job isn't directly related to a social cause, if you focus on the way your job helps people, you might find the kind of inspiration and energy that people such as Jennifer bring to their careers.

Jennifer was hooked on making a difference in her teens and college years. Sometimes she teased her father, a successful CEO, for devoting his life to companies that did mundane things such as make Melba toast. By the time she'd graduated from college, though, Jennifer had changed her tune: "I really saw why what he did was meaningful and how he used his talents." She realized that corporations like the one her father worked for produce important goods and services and provide jobs for people to support their families, send their children to college, and build a society. Business, she saw, wasn't inherently bad. Her father's success impressed her in other ways:

"He influenced me to find what I was good at, something that could contribute to the greater good."

After several years of finding ways to make a mark on the world, Jennifer is a managing director responsible for gender retention and advancement at PricewaterhouseCoopers (PwC). Her work studying social problems and coming up with ways to fix them has already helped change things for the better. Plus, she has a prestigious job and makes a great living. Best of all, Jennifer has a good feeling inside when her young daughter tells people that her mother's job is to help working mothers—and she's providing a secure financial future for herself and her family.

Even if you don't make a career out of bettering the world, you can think of your job—and the good it helps to achieve—as a sort of cause that you're working for. So whether or not you earn money by working for a cause, Jennifer's story shows us all how important it is to rally for a cause.

Starting from Scratch

Fresh out of college with a degree in philosophy, Jennifer needed a job for a year before graduate school. Because she'd been a peer counselor in the dorms at Brown University, dealing with gender issues such as safe sex education and date rape prevention, she figured it might be interesting to do some work related to those causes. She talked to the Dean of Student Affairs and proposed creating a video about safe sex for Brown's undergraduate students.

Jennifer's documentary-style 20-minute video, *Pro's and Condoms,* turned out to be a success. "It was very real and a little funny," Jennifer says. And to this day she still receives royalties from the film distribution company that handles it. But for all the success, it ruled out film as a career for her.

"The actual making of the film wasn't that much fun," Jennifer recalls. Some of the people she worked with were very high maintenance, editing was boring, and the whole process didn't appeal to her. Still, it helped her see that she enjoyed working on projects that helped people live better, safer lives. She just didn't want to be making films about it.

Next, Jennifer went to graduate school. Still looking to work for a cause, she decided on a masters degree in public policy, which is essentially an "MBA for the public sector." She attended the Kennedy School of Government at Harvard University and spent her days studying subjects such as statistics and economics, but instead of talking about the bottom line and increasing profits, the class discussions were about increasing the public good. Jennifer reveled in the discussions and couldn't wait to practice them in the real world. She had just gotten married and planned to move to Washington, D.C. While her husband finished graduate school, Jennifer planned to find a job where she could use what she'd learned about public policy. Little did she know there were things beyond her control that would affect the job market.

Underestimating Obstacles

Jennifer's first obstacle is something we've all heard of: the so-called Republican Revolution in 1994, when the Democratic Party lost its majority in the House and Senate. "People were looking to hire Republicans or people with Republican contacts," recalls Jennifer. "Plus, there were many out-of-work Democrats with more experience than I had." Here she was with a beautiful new degree from Harvard…and she couldn't get a job. She did get interviews and meetings with people, and she got close to getting jobs. But she couldn't make the final cut.

Finally, Jennifer settled for a fundraising job at a gun-control organization earning $30,000, which she considered "almost nothing" given the cost of living in Washington, D.C. As a consolation, she bargained for 6 weeks vacation time—and she got it. With that vacation time, she and her husband planned on going to work as camp counselors over the summer. That way, at least, she could have a little fun and earn some money during the summer.

A lot of people would have felt beaten down at this point, working in a dingy little office in an underpaid job they didn't want. But not Jennifer. She rallied her career and her cause. "I never intended to stay very long," she says. "Gun control really wasn't my issue, but I knew I would learn a lot."

Every job has something it can teach us, no matter how bad it seems. Sometimes, one of the things you learn is what *not* to do. In Jennifer's case, she saw how her gun-control organization was, as she puts it, "totally irrelevant to the national discussion." The group was too far left to have an impact on the national discussion and needed to create middle ground. "I didn't like being at the margins," Jennifer says.

And Jennifer learned another important lesson about rallying for a cause: how to debate and inspire others to follow her. "We were always getting requests to go on right-wing cable television shows for debates," she recalls. "I was lucky to get so much TV experience at 27 years old debating the opposing side." People would call in and say things like, "Little lady, you don't know anything about the second amendment," but Jennifer rallied and stuck with it. "It was a great way to learn how to think on your feet and argue your point in a hostile atmosphere," she says. That skill would get her career moving.

Building Momentum—Optimistically

After one year, Jennifer's upbeat attitude about her less-than-ideal job paid off. The enthusiasm she brought to her gun-control debates on cable TV led her to a new job as a press secretary at SOS (Save Our Strength), an anti-hunger organization. It was a well-respected group that was making a lot of waves in the nonprofit world.

SOS, founded by Bill Shore, was based on the philosophy that for-profit business can be brought into helping the social good. It sounded a lot like what Jennifer had learned from her father—that business wasn't inherently bad and could accomplish good things for society. SOS was a very influential organization that was changing the way nonprofits worked. For example, SOS helped raise money to feed the poor with an event called "Taste of the Nation," where it persuaded restaurants to donate food and skilled chefs to cater events that people would pay $200 a ticket to attend. Plus, big corporations, such as American Express, would agree to sponsor the event and defray costs. "It was a brilliant way to get chefs involved in the hunger issue," Jennifer says. "It was the first time I saw that if you could get a corporation behind something, you could really push your agenda and help people."

After less than a year at SOS, Jennifer's time in D.C. ended. Her husband finished his Ph.D., and the couple moved to New Jersey for his new job and to be closer to her parents. With some great work experience under her belt, Jennifer felt ready to go after the issue she was truly interested in: the advancement of women.

Jennifer landed a job as senior associate for research and consulting at Catalyst, a nonprofit based in New York City that works to increase opportunities for women in business. Its clients are companies that want to retain more women employees and have more women in higher-level leadership. Apparently a big problem in corporate America is that valuable women employees leave right when they're entering their most productive years. A big part of Jennifer's job was researching the question, "Why aren't there more women in corporate leadership?" She interviewed women, surveyed company executives, ran focus groups, and made presentations. "I loved it," Jennifer says. "It used my talents."

One of the best parts was that Jennifer would meet regularly with executives—women and men—and listen to them explain how they achieved success in their fields. The women, especially, gave her insight into what holds women back from reaching the highest levels of leadership and earnings. Jennifer was doing her job, but she was also learning valuable techniques for her own career. "If you listen to all that insight, year after year, you can't help but learn how to manage your own career."

The job at Catalyst also offered Jennifer a flexible schedule, which was important because she and her husband wanted to have children. When her daughter was born, Jennifer returned to work on a 4-day schedule until her daughter was in kindergarten. Jennifer was a walking, talking example of the kinds of things that many women want in order to stay with their employer during their child-bearing years. She was working for a cause that benefited herself as well.

Then, in 2000, PricewaterhouseCoopers became Jennifer's client. The professional services firm had major challenges retaining women, and Jennifer could help. She conducted an assessment of the firm and its policies—trying to get to the root of why women weren't staying at the firm long enough to be promoted to the highest levels.

What she found was that it took a breakneck career pace in order to tough out the first 12 years at PwC, and these were the very years when many young women weren't able to sprint. That's because women who are starting their families often need to take a little time off from their careers. Instead of throwing up her hands at the situation, Jennifer was optimistic that PwC could retain and advance women if they made a few changes. The firm must have been impressed with her ideas because they offered her a job.

Taking the Next Leap

Leaving Catalyst was a hard decision. "It was a huge leap of faith," Jennifer recalls. She would leave a small office where she worked with 64 people who all knew her and move to a place with 30,000 people. What's more, she would be managing a team of 8 people who were in offices all across the country. Her staff would be "virtual reports" who she would keep in touch with through telephone conversations and occasional meetings. That meant longer hours and more travel, and Jennifer was worried about how to balance it all.

Still, Jennifer jumped at the new job. She started out with a chief-of-staff role in the Office of Diversity and threw herself into the task of keeping staff—especially women and minorities—from leaving the firm just when their careers were heating up. The rigid up-or-out model of public accounting didn't work anymore for women or for men.

In order to make changes, Jennifer saw that she would have to sell her solutions to the firm's leadership council, the group of partners that runs the company. She would walk into the room and be faced with two dozen people instead of just one CEO. At times like that, Jennifer says she draws on all the experience she had in the nonprofit world rallying people to her cause.

And she also calls on the research from Catalyst, which found that in order to get ahead in companies, women need to have more "broad" relationships. "Women seem more social, but they treasure intimacy," Jennifer says. "They will have a best friend at work, but business relationships need to be more shallow, broad, and reciprocal. You don't have to like someone to form an alliance at work." So Jennifer works at creating a lot of good will among her colleagues because at some point she knows she'll need it back.

For instance, Jennifer and her team developed a program for women at PwC called Full Circle. Participants are able to leave the firm for up to 5 years in order to parent full-time. They are assigned a coach so they can keep in touch and are brought back for annual training to keep up their technical skills. But first she had to find a way to fund the program. At the beginning, none of the groups she approached wanted to fund it. But Jennifer didn't get mad; she just got creative. To make the program happen, she needed a brochure, website, and money to keep up the training of the women in the program. So she compromised: her team, the Office of Diversity, would pay for the costs of a website and brochure, while the business where the woman worked would pay for ongoing training. After its first year, the program is a success and getting a lot of attention in the media. In fact, PwC has been recognized as a leader in the field of diversity and just won the 2007 Catalyst Award for all its efforts to advance women.

When we feel like the work we do helps make the world a better place, we can dig down deep and find the inspiration we need to move ahead—even during the hard times. As Jennifer puts it: "If you have a great idea and you can mobilize people, you can make great strides."

Wes's Worry Less Tip

► **Change what you can.**

A great deal of business worry comes from wanting everything to be perfect right away. The reality is that the business world doesn't work that way. Instead of worrying about things you can't control, like the economy or job market, do what Jennifer did. Her first job wasn't exactly what she wanted, but she was at peace with that because the job gave her a solid building block for the future. She changed what she could. First by negotiating lots of time off, she was able to supplement her income by doing something she loved and working as a camp counselor. Second, she seized the opportunity at her first job to be a TV spokesperson for the organization's gun control activism. Even though it wasn't the cause she had always dreamed about, it was an extraordinary experience she knew would help her in the future. Like Jennifer, with a little negotiation and thinking on our feet, we can end up getting exactly what we need.

"You can't always get what you want, but if you try sometimes you just might find you get what you need."

—**Rolling Stones**

For more Worry Less Tips, visit www.wesmoss.com.

Part II
Underestimate Your Obstacles

Most people give up too easily. The next principle of the HUNT, Underestimate your obstacles, is about being someone who rarely gives up. It's about being someone who takes a "no" answer with a grain of salt. People in this camp make a practice out of facing every obstacle with the belief that there will always be a solution—no matter what. Whether it's a new job, a bonus, a promotion, or the details of a new project, whenever you hear "no," remember that the world is full of false deadlines and trivial obstacles.

Just as a small business owner has to face hundreds of obstacles to get a business off the ground, we have to face obstacles as we get our careers off the ground. You're not alone in facing the dreaded "no" to your requests; we all face resistance when we try to excel. If you're finding resistance, it means you're on the right path. If it were easy, everyone would find their way to the top! No matter what career or industry you are in, the journey to get to the top will constantly present you with hurdles and challenges. Those who are able to fight through them and find their way around them are the ones who will prevail.

Attitude

Underestimating obstacles doesn't mean that you adopt an idiotic optimism that denies reality; instead, it means having confidence that you'll find a way around difficulty. Sometimes facing difficulty early on can be an advantage. As you saw in Part I, "Harness What You Have," Ralph Olson (Chapter 2, "Embrace Risk") found his strategic advantage in the daily adversity he faced growing up in a gang-ridden urban neighborhood. Olson saw that his disadvantages gave him the advantage over people who had had things given to them—college educations, allowances, and business contacts—by their parents. Because he was used to working for these things, he had confidence that he could overcome whatever obstacles came his way in the work world.

When you're confident about your ability to succeed, you make yourself into a powerful force for an employer. You become known as the person who can get things done—you earn respect and attention.

Raise the Bar

Everyone in this book overcame challenges and sought out more in their lives, but the stories in Part II are especially compelling. Kevin Noland figured career growth wasn't happening fast enough at GE, so he went to a small company with fast-moving career paths and begged for a job. Dan Pelson didn't have the computer engineering degree everyone said he needed, but he got into the information technology industry anyway. Steve Hudson lived through a car accident that could have killed him and made it through an industry contraction that could have hurt his career. Diana Ruddick pushed through her boss's refusal to promote women and then turned around and helped her company modernize and open itself to providing more opportunities for women. When these folks didn't have enough challenges, they chased more.

What challenges could you tackle right now in your career? As you read this book, ask yourself that question and envision pushing right through these challenges. The stories in this book can help you do that.

Don't Underestimate Your Competition

I put this in because I'm constantly surprised (and I'm sure you've seen this) by people who come to sell me things but don't want to answer any tough questions. For instance, wholesalers representing different investment-related products will lobby for me to use their products or investment vehicle for my clients. But for example, when I ask why their costs are higher than their main competition, the only answer is, "We're so confident that we're the best that we don't even know exactly what the competition is offering"—sounds like they are either lazy or not willing to answer the tough questions with an honest response!

So be sure you know what your company's competitors—or your competitors in the office—are up to. And think through why your ideas—or your company's products—are better than someone else's. When you're selling yourself (or your company), it pays to prepare answers to the most difficult questions. Not only does it make you look smart and well-prepared, it also cuts down on worry. After you have answers for the all the tough questions, there's nothing further to worry about!

Push the Envelope

Just because something hasn't been done before doesn't mean you can't try it. There's no such thing as a stupid idea: Look at the *Teenage Mutant Ninja Turtles*, a hugely successful children's cartoon. It's an utterly ridiculous idea; turtles are one of the slowest creatures around, yet the idea to use them as fearless heroes appealed to children and was marketed brilliantly. If that idea can fly, anything can become a success.

This is one of the keys to solving challenges—coming up with new ways to do things. You don't have to come up with a new cartoon or the next Post-it note, just consider trying a new tactic that's used in another industry. For instance, women's advisory groups had been around in other industries, but no one at Diana Ruddick's company (Chapter 9, "Command Attention") had heard about them before; when she got these groups going, she doubled the pool of recruits in a career that had previously appealed mostly to men. That earned her the eternal gratitude of her boss and added to her clout in the company. Perhaps there's a technology or marketing idea that has not yet been adopted at your company; it could provide answers to a host of problems—and get you noticed!

That's why it's always smart to be well-read and up to date with what the heck is going on in the world. Read magazines to find out what's going on in the business world; stay informed about what innovators in your industry are up to. It's also a great idea to go to industry conferences and training because you will see things other companies are trying that your company doesn't know about. Wars have been won and lost over only slight information advantages. Knowledge is power—so make sure you have some!

Mistakes Are Inevitable

Just because things don't always work out doesn't mean you were on the wrong track. There are a million reasons why things fail—and they're not always your fault. And even if it is your fault, learn from your mistake. As you'll see in Part III, "Notice Your Work," Ralph Stayer (Chapter 10, "The Butterfly Effect") doesn't fail an employee who makes a mistake—even if it costs the company money. His philosophy is that if he fires someone who's made a mistake, he loses his investment in that person's education; it's only when people don't learn from mistakes that he considers firing them. The opportunity to make mistakes and learn from them is an intangible compensation of having a job. Learn from your mistakes.

Survive

No one wins every battle. When you're down and out—without a job or heading a doomed project—remember that you can always salvage something. Most of the people in this book have had huge setbacks, yet they survived to tackle other challenges and win other battles. If your job or career is filled with challenges right now, you may consider that a good sign. When things are going smoothly for too long, it's a sign you're not being challenged. If you are experiencing a set back right now—learn from it! After you weather the present circumstances, material success could be right around the corner!

Here are the hallmarks of people who underestimate their obstacles:

- They have a "can do" attitude, looking at problems as new opportunities to shine.
- They raise the bar. When things are going well, they challenge themselves.
- They push the envelope. Just because something has never been done doesn't mean it can't be done.
- They realize mistakes are inevitable.
- They survive to fight another day. Even when they lose a battle, they learn and triumph in the future.

Wes's Worry Less Tip

► Conquer worry with the worst-case scenario.

I don't discount the power of positive thinking, but at the same time there's something extremely powerful about accepting the worst and building from there. Most of the subjects in this book talked about using this coping tool to help them minimize their worries. For example, Dan Pelson (Chapter 7, "See Around the Corner") has an exciting and successful career in the music and recording industry. Yet he told me that when he starts to worry about his career he imagines that if things totally went sour and he lost *everything*, he could always go back to his first job of being a waiter. This worst-case scenario thinking has a way of cutting our worries down to size. No matter what happens to our careers, all of us can always rebound. This kind of thinking—imagining the worst-case scenario—has a way of taking the worry out of everyday challenges.

Dale Carnegie has an extreme example of this in his book *How to Stop Worrying and Start Living*.[1] He tells the story of Earl Haney, who was on his deathbed due to stomach ulcers caused by worry. Haney's worries led to such debilitating stomach problems, that his doctor told him that he was sure to die of bleeding ulcers. Finally, he figured instead of facing an agonizing and lingering death he would take a cruise and enjoy what time he had left. Haney boarded a ship, loaded his own coffin aboard, and was determined to enjoy his last weeks. Then something interesting happened; after he accepted his fast-approaching death, he completely stopped worrying. Why worry about *anything* he thought, if there was NOTHING he could do to prevent it? Miraculously he recovered! With his mental anguish and worry stripped away, his body was finally able to heal. What's more, he extended the cruise and visited ports in developing parts of the world where rampant poverty made his business worries look miniscule. He returned from the cruise a healthy man with a healthy outlook on life.

[1] Carnegie, Dale, *How to Stop Worrying and Start Living.* New York: Simon and Schuster, 1984.

Try worst-case scenario thinking the next time you're beset by worries about your career or your finances. The reason this is so important is if we're not mired down with worry about setbacks, which are inevitable in business, then we're more able to function at our full potential. As long as you can accept the worst-case scenario, things can only get better from there.

"True peace of mind comes from accepting the worst."

—**Lin Yutang, Chinese author,** *Importance of Living*

For more Worry Less Tips, visit www.wesmoss.com.

6

Be Distinct or Be Extinct

—Kevin Noland (A.D.A.M., Inc.)

Talking with Kevin Noland is like drinking a double shot of espresso at an amusement park. He's just plain exciting. That's because Kevin is the kind of guy who sees the fun in things rather than the downside. It started when Kevin was a teen and wanted to be an edgy rock star and moved to Atlanta to get discovered—and just to play it safe he enrolled in engineering school. Obviously, Kevin never became a rock star, but he thrived in buckled-down corporate America in a way you wouldn't expect: He made himself *stand out* instead of *fitting in.*

"I never wanted a job. I wanted an adventure," Kevin says. Yet even though corporate jobs aren't usually considered chock-full of adventure, Kevin took his long hair and rocker image and got on the corporate career path shortly after college. It started with computer programming. Intrigued by IBM's Personal Computers, Kevin taught himself computer programming in college. So instead of using his industrial engineering degree after graduation, Kevin and one of his professors started a little shoestring computer programming business. It was 1984, when typewriters and calculators were still standard office equipment, and computer programming skills were pretty rare. After a couple years, Kevin found himself working at GE on consulting gigs week after week. Brushing shoulders with high-powered executives, Kevin started to see that GE was a pretty exciting place. When the company offered him a job as a programmer, Kevin took it.

Here is what's so important about Kevin's story: Even though he left an entrepreneurial venture to take a corporate job, Kevin never left the sense of adventure he got from having his own startup computer programming business. After all, there's no shame in not starting your own company—or starting a company and bailing out—because being on your own is *hard*. Owning your own company has plenty of rewards, but it's not for everyone. That's why I wrote this book: Many people want to adopt an entrepreneurial attitude while working for a steady paycheck because the tough thing about starting your own business is the money risk. "You really had to go fight for every dollar," Kevin recalls of his days trying to build his own computer consulting business. Right out of college in his early 20s, Kevin could get along on $50 a week by splitting rent with several roommates. But GE's offer of stability and a paycheck was too good to turn down.

What Kevin found during the course of his career is that he could be distinct—*needed* to be distinct—even in the corporate world. Instead of complaining about the structure of a 9-to-5 job in a huge corporation, Kevin embraced it as yet another adventure. And he took the famous quote of management guru Tom Peters and made it his own mantra: "Be *distinct* or be *extinct*."

Starting from Scratch

Right off, Kevin was immersed in computer programming projects using dBASE, an early programming product for the PC, which was quickly becoming standard office equipment. These were the days before Microsoft Windows, when you looked at a computer screen and all you saw was a blinking green dot. "If you didn't know how to talk to the dot, it did nothing," Kevin says. "It gave you an immense feeling of power. No one knew how to make the dot work unless he was a programmer. This was all cutting-edge stuff at the time."

At first, Kevin figured he might spend his whole career at GE; just like the man who sat in the next cubicle, a chain-smoking engineer (you could still smoke at your desk back then) who was getting ready to retire after working at GE since he was 18 years old. It was a time when Jack Welch was CEO of GE and was "gardening" the company's future leadership; Kevin saw so many opportunities. Working in upstate New York at GE's information services group, he enrolled in the management training program, quickly moved up from programmer to project manager, and eventually became manager to some of his former cubicle mates, including the chain-smoking engineer. "It was a pretty cool experience," Kevin says. "Plus, I knew even then that this opportunity would translate into a great foundation for doing things later."

Then came a life-changing moment. You know the kind—one of those quirky moments that comes along and that make you stop, think, and change direction. Kevin had one of those moments while flipping through a dBASE handbook at work one day. It started with the phrase "endless loop," which is when a computer program repeats an operation over and over. In the handbook glossary the term "endless loop" was defined simply as "see: loop, endless." Then, under the term "loop, endless" the definition was "see: endless loop." It was a clever joke that made the handbook user flip back and forth between the two definitions and *experience* an endless loop. Kevin was amazed that a company would put a humorous bit like that into a handbook. "I thought it was the coolest thing," he recalls. Suddenly, Kevin knew he wouldn't stay at GE all his life, and he wouldn't go back to starting his own company. What he wanted was to work for the company that *made* dBASE.

"You have to seek out your passion; otherwise, your career moves become dead ends," Kevin says. Even though GE gave him great opportunities to learn management skills and planning, Kevin felt his passion for the job growing cold. "It wasn't entrepreneurial enough," he says.

In 1989, in his late 20s, Kevin contacted Ashton-Tate, the company that made dBASE, and told them he would come and sweep the floors if they would just hire him. It was a funny thing to say, and it set him apart from other programmers who were asking for a job. And his experience at GE also set him apart. Luckily, he could leave his broom at home; Ashton-Tate hired Kevin on as programmer, and he was off to the West Coast for another adventure.

Underestimating Obstacles

Instead of hanging around the office writing code, Kevin saw that the real fun was going along on sales calls. He did this a few times, working as a "sales engineer" who showed the prospective customer how the product worked. "I was the guy they put in front of the crowd," Kevin says. As Kevin demonstrated dBASE, the sales guys— who stood to earn big commissions if the sale closed—sat around and watched. When Kevin realized the sales reps were making ten times more money than him, he asked to move to sales: "I've got the knowledge; I want the money," he told his boss. And into sales he went— becoming one of the few sales reps who could actually use Ashton-Tate's products.

I love how Kevin negotiated that obstacle and set himself apart: When he saw that he wasn't earning commission, he went ahead and asked for the job. Notice that he didn't just gripe and moan. Another thing he didn't do: He didn't come into the company and ask right away to be in sales. Kevin simply got his foot in the door as a programmer, demonstrated his valuable knowledge about the dBASE product, and then asked for the lucrative sales position. The Ashton-Tate people got a taste of what he could do for them, so they gladly put him in sales—and why not? He would be putting more money in their pockets if he stayed in sales anyway.

Then came another type of obstacle: consolidation. One by one, software makers were merging with or acquiring one another. Ashton-Tate was purchased by Borland International, a Silicon Valley rival, and Kevin had to deal with a different kind of corporate culture. Even though he did well at Borland, becoming one of the top sales producers, Kevin was restless for more adventure. So after putting in a few years at Borland, he went on to a small software company in Beaverton, Oregon, called Central Point Software, which was acquired within just a year by Symantec.

"Each one of those experiences I approached as if it were the next rung in the ladder," Kevin recalls. "I looked at it as adding another layer of experience." But hopping around to different employers and having them acquired by a different company every few months was taking its toll. "Two cultures clashing, it's always hard," Kevin recalls. Plus, he was living part-time on the West Coast and trying to make a home on the East Coast where he lived with his wife in Atlanta. It was all too hectic.

Probably plenty of people in the technology world were also unhappy with the climate of consolidation, but unlike Kevin they didn't feel like there was anything they could do about it. Kevin *did* something. He'd heard of a software company in Atlanta called A.D.A.M. Inc., which was doing some interesting things. In fact, he'd once been recruited by A.D.A.M. and turned down the job. But his frustration on the West Coast made him take a second look at A.D.A.M., and he liked what he saw: "I thought it was just the coolest company I'd ever seen," Kevin says. It had an intriguing product that reminded him of his Ashton-Tate days. Even though he wouldn't be earning sales commission, he would be learning something new: marketing.

Building Momentum—Virtually

There's something about looking at anatomy drawings that really pulls you in. That's why people love to page through the classic color illustrations of Gray's *Anatomy of the Human Body*. A.D.A.M.'s main product went one step better than an anatomy book: It was a three-dimensional virtual human body. Medical students could use it to virtually dissect a human cadaver, and people with a passing interest in anatomy loved it too. Kevin knew it was a great product. And at A.D.A.M. they had doctors and medical illustrators with fine art backgrounds—people who really treated the illustrations with care. Plus they had great software to navigate the illustrations. Kevin dug in.

"It was really the most exciting place I'd ever worked," Kevin recalls. The combination of working with doctors, medical illustrators, fine artists, and scientists was fascinating to him. "It was so different from what I was used to selling, like databases and other IT products," Kevin says. At this point, money was not his main motivator. At A.D.A.M., Kevin was working in marketing and not earning sales commissions like he had on the West Coast. What he had was that ever-important sense of adventure. So he immersed himself in A.D.A.M.'s main product, the virtual human body.

"I just knew with the proper kind of market opportunity this company could be something totally different," Kevin says. At the time, it was a small, privately owned company with about 40 employees. Since A.D.A.M. needed capital to grow, the founder decided to raise money with a public offering in 1995.

In the mid-1990s, computers were just coming out with CD-ROM drives, and people were hungry to buy disks to put in those drives. "Retail software was a very hot category," Kevin remembers. So with plenty of money in the bank, A.D.A.M. threw its business into producing retail CD-ROM versions of the A.D.A.M. virtual body for home users. A.D.A.M. had fantastic production capability and a unique market niche. But by the Christmas season of 1995, the market was already saturated: Instead of selling for $50 apiece, A.D.A.M.'s discs were ending up in the sale bargain bin.

So Kevin, who was just a cubicle dweller in the marketing department, walked over to the company founder and chairman, Bob Cramer, and told him, "A.D.A.M. should get out of the retail market and this is why...." A lot of people might not go out on a limb like that, but Kevin wasn't trying to be like everyone else. He was just calling it like he saw it. Impressed by his honesty, Cramer agreed.

"All of a sudden we had to revamp the company," recalls Kevin. By now, Kevin was used to underestimating obstacles, and he'd made a name for himself as a straight-talker. He took everything he'd learned so far in his career and searched for a way to make A.D.A.M. different from all the other ailing software retailers.

Taking the Next Leap

In the mid-1990s, buzz about the Internet was growing. Consumers were learning to do things such as order pizza off the Pizza Hut website and use online banks. In the middle of all this buzz, A.D.A.M. took its encyclopedia of symptoms and diseases and hooked it up to the Internet—just to see what would happen. Even at a time when most people didn't have an Internet connection, the site became a traffic magnet, taking hundreds of hits a day. The host that ran the site was an old Macintosh at A.D.A.M.'s headquarters that was set up in one of the cubicles. "Every day we would walk by that cube and say, 'There's got to be a business there,'" Kevin recalls.

It turns out that health information—right up there with pornography and financial information—is one of the top three topics researched on the Internet. Who knew? No one, and that's the point. In the brave new world of the Internet, new business models were being created every day. It was incredibly exciting. Kevin and his team transformed the company into ADAM.com and made it a destination site for healthcare information.

Kevin, who had never really worked in marketing, put together a
hilarious marketing stunt. He hired beautiful models—male and
female—to fly around the country on airplanes wearing only skintight bodysuits painted to look like they were wearing nothing but a
few fig leaves. At an IT industry event, the models walked around the
convention center with apples *a la* the biblical story of Adam and Eve.
A.D.A.M. got noticed, even though the models were thrown out of
the convention center for being too provocative. And it wasn't just the
ADAM.com site that was making money; the company was also supplying health content to most of its competitors, such as Web MD and
Dr.Koop.com.

Just as A.D.A.M.'s stock price climbed, the dot-com market
blew up.

Unlike a lot of other dot-coms, however, A.D.A.M. had plenty of
money in the bank from its initial public offering and time to come up
with a plan to stay afloat. In 2000, Kevin remembers the company
founder came to him and asked him to retool the company.

"We had to quickly do something," says Kevin, who still has flashback anxiety to those days. "'Man,' I thought, 'here we go again.'" The
solution? Go after the healthcare market.

Usually when a company revamps, it brings in a Harvard MBA or
McKinsey consultants. But Kevin had a reputation as an independent
thinker with a zest for solving problems—no MBA needed. "It's not
that hard," Kevin says about retooling the company. "The simple rule
is you don't spend more than you make. You do more with less, and
you invest in the things that give you the greatest return."

Since 2001, A.D.A.M. has been selling annual contracts to hospitals, HMOs, and drug makers that use A.D.A.M.'s healthcare content
to connect people to their websites. As Kevin climbed the executive
ranks, he wasn't afraid to ask for what he wanted. One day 4 years ago,
Kevin was helping the head of human resources with a job description

handbook and read the description of Chief Operating Officer, a position that A.D.A.M. didn't have. He was incredulous because the title described everything that he did, and he was only a vice president. "I definitely had to ask for that COO title," Kevin recalls. "I went into Bob's office and said, 'That's what I need to be.' He was for it."

A few years later, in 2006, Kevin's title had to catch up with him again. He was named CEO because he was doing all the jobs that went into it.

All along the way, Kevin made himself distinct by not being afraid to speak his mind—and by being willing to think creatively instead of falling back on a tired business model. "Most people walk through life asleep," Kevin says. There are plenty of opportunities for people who keep their eyes open.

Kevin's story shows us how to distinguish ourselves by picking up experience along the way—not by having the right business school pedigree—and how to set ourselves apart from the crowd. Which just goes to show that it's easier to be a CEO than it is to become a rocker! And maybe just as fun.

Be Distinct (Not Extinct)

Kevin has some great tips for distinguishing yourself that are indispensable for corporate climbers:

- Have an adventure by doing work that is interesting to you rather than work that everyone else thinks you should do. Don't take a job for the money; take a job to put the next arrow in your quiver.
- Keep learning new skills.
- Earn a reputation for speaking your mind and delivering the goods, not being a suck-up.
- Look for chances to be a change agent for your company.
- When you distinguish yourself by making a great contribution, don't hesitate to ask to take the next step.

Wes's Worry Less Tip

► Take your medicine.

Facing reality can be a difficult pill to swallow, but it allows you to live worry free. Kevin was good at facing reality—and letting his boss know how he saw things. He could have placated his boss and ignored that his company's business model was becoming irrelevant; instead Kevin called it like he saw it. His honesty earned him the right to lead the company forward into profitability. There's a power in getting something off your chest; not only are you telling the truth to yourself, you're telling the truth to your colleagues. Just as when you ignore a disease it only gets worse, ignoring problems is deadly. Lying to yourself or placating your boss and walking on eggshells just isn't worth the anxiety. If you address problems before they get bigger, your worries will shrink. Even if what you have to say isn't going to make people happy, in the long run you're making for a lot less worry. Try it yourself: think of something you should admit to yourself or point out to someone else. Start small and see how much more relaxed you feel when you take your medicine and face reality.

"Peace of mind is gained not by ignoring problems but by solving them."

—Raymond Hull, coauthor of *The Peter Principle*

7

See Around the Corner

—Dan Pelson (Warner Music Group)

Where were you when the digital revolution hit? Maybe you were too young to remember, or maybe you were busy making a living. Dan Pelson knows just where he was: sitting on his front steps reading *Wired* magazine's cover article about Mosaic, which was a new web browser at the time. Mosaic, the first popular web browser, made the Internet accessible for regular folks. That was in 1993. Dan sat there reading about it and said, "This is incredible!" And he knew he had to find a way to be a part of it. Dan is the kind of person who has that uncanny ability to see around corners and make a pretty accurate guess about where business is going—accurate enough for Warner Music Group to hire him on as a senior vice president to remake their Internet marketing business.

Dan's 20-year career in the ever-evolving digital media industry shows that you don't really have to have superpowers to see where business is going; you just have to be a little less skeptical than everyone else. When Dan had his awakening about the Internet, he was busy selling servers for Sun Microsystems, his first real job after college. It was a pretty good job, and he did well at it. But here he was, knocking on doors, persuading publications such as *Time* to digitize their magazines instead of laying them out by cutting and pasting on paper. While *Time* bosses were puzzling over how to make use of computers, Dan already saw the possibilities of the new technology to revolutionize media. "I literally woke up in the middle of the night," he recalls, "and I said, 'Why am I evangelizing to media companies when there's this huge revolution coming with digital content?'"

Even though Dan's career is a mix of working for corporations and running his own businesses, I include Dan in this book because he's a great example of how to manage your career in a time when change is inevitable. In the past 10 years, your employer has probably tweaked its business model to adapt to the digital world. I guarantee your company will keep tweaking its business model, and maybe change it totally, thanks to the Internet and information technology. We can dread the changes and how they affect our jobs, or we can see the opportunities. People like Dan who see the opportunities of the future will be rewarded.

Forward-thinking people who profit off change have a common characteristic: They trust their judgment. Dan wasn't the only person reading the *Wired* cover story about the new web browser, but not everyone who read that article came to the same realization as he did. Dan wasn't writing software like Steve Jobs and Bill Gates, and he didn't make computers—he just sold them. He simply knew how to use a computer and how it could be used to do things such as stream-line publishing. The new Mosaic browser showed him that instead of just streamlining conventional publishing, the Internet would do away with magazines or at least create a new kind of magazine— the e-zine.

That's the thing about seeing around corners: We have to believe in our hunches. If you're working today, you have inside information about whatever industry your employer happens to be in. Learn all you can about that industry, and you might be surprised at the insights you come up with. Dan's confidence in his vision of what's around the corner led him on a whirlwind career.

Starting from Scratch

Dan graduated from Colgate University with a liberal arts degree in 1988. When it came to a career, he wanted to jump on the digital bandwagon because it was the next new thing. Sun Microsystems was growing like crazy, hiring 40 people a week, and Dan wanted to work there. Even though he didn't have an engineering degree, he was persistent. "I basically told them I'd work for free to get there," says Dan, who downplays that achievement. "They just needed go-getters at the time to help them through a rapid period of growth."

For the first year, he was part of the marketing team: "Driving a van around for company trade shows," Dan says. What he really wanted to do was get into sales, but Sun was concentrating its efforts on selling to rocket scientists at Los Alamos Labs and derivatives traders on Wall Street. These were sophisticated people, so most of the sales staff had computer engineering degrees. Still, Dan kept asking to get into sales.

After a year, he got his wish. Sun executives were broadening their sales strategy and looking beyond the traditional markets. "There's only so many computers you can sell to laboratories and Wall Street, although they sold a hell of a lot of computers to Wall Street," Dan says. "They figured, 'Let's take the kid and throw him into media and have him try to break in.'" So Dan got into a brand-new sales vertical, making his rounds to print media outlets Such as *Time*, Dow Jones, and McGraw-Hill, showing publishers how computers could streamline production.

Back in those days, newspapers and magazines were laid out by first typing articles into large mainframes, printing them out, and then handing over the contents to a graphic arts department that literally cut and pasted everything together. Graphics were drawn by hand on paper, although some publishers were just starting to have their graphic arts people play with Macintosh computers to get some interesting graphics. Still, the work was printed out and then cut and pasted together by hand with scissors and glue.

To sell to the publishing industry, Dan used tried-and-true sales techniques. "You pick up the phone and try to track down leads. There's no real magic to it," he says. "In 4 years I had a tremendous amount of success. The timing was great." Sony Music bought huge servers to keep track of royalties, Associated Press bought servers to tabulate election accounting results on election night, HBO started using Sun's system and would buy hundreds of workstations and servers. These were the days when businesses were building their computer infrastructure nearly from the ground up, transferring information from mainframes to smaller units.

And these were still the pre-Internet days. Although the Internet existed, it was mainly used by scientists. Web pages were utilitarian looking with just text and no graphics. Individuals couldn't even access the Web from home computers, if they were one of the few households who owned a computer. Then, suddenly, things changed.

In 1993, a new web browser, Mosaic, was released. *Wired*, a new magazine at the time, ran the cover article about Mosaic that got Dan excited. Here he was telling *Time* to lay out their magazines on computers instead of cutting and pasting with paper. Then this article forecasts that more and more people would have home computers linked up through the World Wide Web. It wasn't hard for Dan to go one step further and see that if magazines were laid out on paper, that meant they could be linked to consumers' home computers through the World Wide Web using a browser such as Mosaic.

Dan saw around the corner, and he was so excited he decided to start up his own online magazine.

In case you are thinking of going out on your own 100%, visit www.wesmoss.com for more information on my first book, *Starting from Scratch*.

Underestimating Obstacles

Again, Dan's timing was great. He quit Sun on December 31, 1993, and launched his e-zine—*Word*—on January 1, 1994. In 1994, online services started popping up, and computers with modems were becoming standard. His e-zine was a simple website aimed at young adults in their 20s, just like Dan. It was full of articles that he and a few friends wrote about how to cope with life after college. "The content was probably not the best," he says.

"But the Web was just coming to public consciousness—us and Yahoo were the first two places you could actually place advertising on the Web."

Word didn't make him rich, but it did get him a job in the emerging e-zine market. Remember that launching a little shoestring business was also how Kevin Noland got his job at GE as a computer programmer, even without a programming degree. I'm not saying that you have to necessarily launch your own company, but it's interesting how when new technology comes out, companies are eager to hire employees with nontraditional backgrounds.

Dan got hired at Icon CMT Corp., a technology company whose main income stream came from providing bandwidth to companies. Icon acquired *Word* and hired him to build its brand-new media practice. Dan and his little staff at *Word* all joined Icon. Here was Dan, just a few years out of college, and he was running the new media practice at a technology company. Over the next few years, he'd grown the group into a staff of 75 people. Besides *Word*, they also put out another e-zine, *Charge*, aimed at extreme sports types. It became a large operation for the time, generating revenue from ads. "It was an exciting time. It was generating a lot of interest, and things were going great," Dan says.

This was in 1996, just before Icon went public. Even though his media group was chugging along, Dan ran into a difference of opinion with the Icon founder. Since his group was so successful, he wanted to spin out his group into another company. Icon's founder disagreed, so Dan left. As he tells it, this wasn't a difficult decision because, again, he had an idea what was coming around the corner. Online media was where the action would be, he believed, and there was no doubt in his mind that pursuing that wholeheartedly would be a better move than staying with Icon, where media was a sideline. "*Word* had given me a lot of recognition, so I was able to raise a million bucks to get the company off the ground," Dan says. "It wasn't that difficult."

Building Momentum—Persistently

On his own again in 1996, Dan called his new company Concrete Media. The idea was to design and maintain websites for brick and mortar companies that were just establishing their websites. Concrete Media also had its own online media—a site called Bolt, a social networking site for teens. Bolt was making money from ads, and Concrete Media was making money from selling online services and building websites and portals. To add to the media content, Dan also purchased a small movie review website called Girls on Film (clean movies—not what you were thinking!). The company grew to more than 400 employees.

Things were going so well that by 1999 Dan was getting ready to take Bolt (the social networking site) public. Morgan Stanley was the company's bank, and by November 2000 it had filed plans for an initial public offering (IPO). In April 2000, Bolt planned a road show to promote its coming IPO; that was the same month the dot-com bubble burst, and no one wanted to buy stock in a technology company. Things went from great to horrible in 1 month, and of course, there was no IPO for Bolt. This was the beginning of the end for Concrete Media.

When Dan talks about those times, he's very calm; but it must have been horrible. "After the market crashed, the Internet was viewed as a fad," Dan remembers. "People were saying, 'Is the Internet going to survive?'" The *Wall Street Journal* called the Web the "CB radio of the 1990s." Concrete Media's business went down the drain because no one was paying to launch new websites, and advertising revenue went down at Bolt—but it didn't completely dry up. Bolt's business kept afloat, hanging on by a thread, but Dan still saw possibility and profitability in the Internet, and he sat tight.

The business climate got even worse. What remained of Bolt and Concrete Media were housed in Manhattan, and on September 11th, most of his employees were at work and saw the World Trade Center terrorist attack (Dan happened to be on the West Coast). "It added tremendously to the challenge of keeping people motivated after the dot-com bubble burst," says Dan, who kept himself focused on the benefit Bolt brought to the millions of teens who came to the site. As we see in many of the stories in this book, when times get hard, focusing on the social benefit of your work can keep you going.

"Millions of teens were coming to the site every month, and you don't want to just walk away from that. I had dedicated, passionate employees, and I didn't want to walk away from them either. I kind of felt we had to do everything we could to survive, and we deserved to survive." Did he ever doubt that he could continue? "Every day," Dan says.

Even though Bolt's advertisers had cut back, it was as popular as ever with teens. "I felt like they needed us more than ever," he says. "Having a social network is about expressing yourself and having a forum to do that in. For me, personally, I realized it was going to be a long time coming before Bolt was a substantial value again." Just before its IPO plans, Bolt was valued at $350 million. After the crash there wasn't even a value placed on it; it wasn't clear that there could be a financial return.

Then, by 2004, advertisers were back, some great Internet companies were launched (Google, for example), and the Internet was back in style. Bolt got back some of its advertisers and became profitable again. Dan brought in his old partner, Aaron Cohen, and sold Bolt. During that time he also sold Girls on Film, something he'd bought for a few thousand dollars, to Oxygen Media for several million.

Why not stay at the helm of Bolt? "I kind of got itchy about hanging onto the company for 10 years," he says. "I wanted to do other things." Dan didn't earn the huge fortune that had dangled in front of him before the dot-com bubble burst, but he did earn a small fortune from the sale of Girls on Film. "Compared to most people, I feel really lucky," he says.

Taking the Next Leap

As he figured out his next step, Dan took a year off. He chilled out, got married, and had a baby. "Running a business, it's kind of hard to have a relationship with anyone," says Dan, who really needed that year off. "I don't look back and say I lost a year. I needed to think about myself for a little while."

To get back into the job market, Dan consulted for 6 months for Evite. "It wasn't big enough to get me fired up," Dan says, so he declined their job offer. Then he thought about how he'd always loved music. Along with his friend Bo Peabody, Dan started a website, UPlayMe, that connects people with people who are downloading and listening to the same music. "It becomes a social network of music lovers," Dan says. "Pulling people together through entertainment and making it a social experience again."

A few months into UPlayMe, Warner Music Group came knocking. The company wanted Dan to remake its 1,000-plus high-traffic artist websites to keep up with the changes hitting the music industry. Dan says it has been easy to maneuver the corporate waters because he has a track record of building profitable websites. He just thinks of his chunk of Warner as a great big startup instead of a media conglomerate and feels the same kind of ownership as he does with his own businesses. "I'm helping the company completely reinvent their business model," he says. "So that part is very entrepreneurial. The transition hasn't been that difficult."

Dan says the main problem he sees in corporations is the fear of risk: "I've left meetings where there was discussion and debate and argument over which path to take. Guys who've been here 10 years say, 'Oh my God, I hope you have a job after that one.' I know they're joking, but I'm shocked that that's even on their minds. That's just the course of normal business, to get into debate, argue, and get passionate about this stuff. If that's *not* happening, they should be worried about their jobs. It's a volatile chaotic time in the music industry. We're trying to be transformative and effective."

One of the biggest obstacles is that music artists aren't accustomed to seeing advertising on their websites. But with 15 million unique visitors around the world, "Of course we should be putting advertising on these sites. That's a whole new revenue stream for us!" Dan says. "I know we have to maintain that artist relationship, but if 5 years from now we're still generating income from that artist, we're going to have a better shot at maintaining that artist relationship than the way we've been doing business."

Dan's main challenge now is to change the industry from being focused on artists into being focused on consumers. Instead of just packaging music and using the websites to get people to buy CDs at brick and mortar stores, the websites need to offer more. "You've got a lot of traffic coming, and these are very passionate people visiting these websites."

"Business models at every major media company are definitely going to change," says Dan, peeking around the corner again. "Warner has accepted that need to change. Now the question is how to transform the organization to make it happen."

Whatever your industry, how do you use Dan's advice to position yourself to take advantage of the inevitable changes hitting business every day? "You have to be willing to take risks," Dan advises. From his point of view, not taking a risk is the more risky path. Whether Dan's vision of the media business is right or wrong, he's getting rewarded for his vision today. And if he's even a little right, he'll be rewarded again the next time people need to see what's coming around the corner.

If we try to adapt parts of Dan's approach even a little bit and trust our view of what's happening in our industries, we can be sure to benefit in some way. If we do nothing, we're sure to miss out. Try looking around the next corner today and see how you like the view.

How to See Around the Corner

In today's world of constant change, looking ahead is an important habit. Dan breaks it down to some simple, common-sense steps:

- If you already have a job, look at the industry you're working in for signs of change; read industry magazines and blogs and talk to people about what they see.
- Trust your judgment when you see changes happening.
- Position yourself to take advantage of the changes; you don't have to start your own company, just be sure your skills are in line with the new wave.
- Volunteer to work on projects in your job where the changes are happening.

Wes's Worry Less Tip

► Know you're not perfect.

Most people worry when it comes to presenting their new ideas to their boss. So the next time you have to make a presentation, be sure to use Dan's trick: Ask yourself the tough questions. After all, there's no such thing as a perfect plan or a perfect person. You need to be incredibly honest with yourself about the flaws in what you're presenting. Many people don't want to accept that they don't have perfect answers for every issue, so they don't rehearse the tough questions. Meanwhile, deep inside they know it's an obvious question to ask. That knowledge rumbles inside their gut, and they feel worried. If you're honest with yourself about the weakest points of your plan or presentation, you can think through how to answer any questions about them! Not only will you feel more confident, but your presentation will be much more believable. Also when worries mount, Dan says a scotch never hurts…

"Face reality as it is, not as it was or as you wish it to be."

—Jack Welch

8

Chart Your Course

—Steve Hudson (Omnilink Systems)

To all the midlevel managers stuck in a cubicle somewhere slaving for a chance at promotion, Steve Hudson's story gives hope—and direction! Steve is great at analyzing career moves. His biggest discovery was that sometimes a promotion is *not* the best thing for your career.

Promotions, after all, aren't there to help your career; they're there to help the company achieve its goals. You have to evaluate and analyze your company's promotion record and see where you're headed, even if you are in a management trainee program. Instead of hoping for promotion, Steve's story encourages us to skillfully chart our career course like the captain on a ship. Sometimes you'll get busy hauling in fish and working hard, but every now and then you have to look at the stars and navigate those corporate waters. After years in corporate jobs, Steve analyzed his situation, and instead of angling for promotion, he tried something very different. Steve opted to become vice president of business development at a smaller technology startup.

Wasn't he taking a big risk by leaving a big corporate employer? No, he says, because he came to see that moving down to a small company just as his career was heating up was actually less risky than staying put at Sprint PCS. "My mentor told me, 'It would probably be more of a risk for you to stay than to go to a small company,'" Steve recalls. That's because, as Sprint PCS went through several rounds of layoffs, Steve saw great people let go. Telecom was becoming a commodity, and margins were shrinking. So when the offer came for vice president of business development at Omnilink Systems, Steve jumped for it; and he hasn't looked back since!

I Wanna Be Like Steve!

Here's the important thing: Every industry is different. You don't need to copy Steve's career moves. What we could all emulate, though, is the way he analyzes and takes stock of his career instead of just blindly hoping his company will take care of him. It's not enough to have a 10-year plan. Steve says that the important thing to consider is, "Are you doing the right things today to get yourself where you want to be in 10 years?"

Steve's analytical style isn't limited to his career. He and his wife went to *three* premarital counseling sessions *before* they got married. They wanted to be sure that they could handle the hurdles of a mixed-faith marriage. I'm not suggesting everyone change their personality and become as analytical as Steve, but his style of taking stock of his career every year and making adjustments is a great idea that everyone can use.

Starting from Scratch

In the late 1980s, telecom was king. The industry had just been deregulated; in a battle over market share, telecom carriers waged aggressive telemarketer campaigns to persuade households to switch their long distance carriers. Both Steve's parents had jobs at Sprint, a telecom giant. Telecommunications, Steve figured, would be his industry. "To me, this is what I do. It's what we talked about at the dinner table," he says.

Early in his college years, Steve had an experience that might be the reason he's so careful and analytical. His freshman year at the University of Kansas, he joined a fraternity and lived in a house where he admittedly "had a little too much fun." That spring he went on a road trip to visit a friend and was a passenger in a horrific car accident. "I was with a fraternity brother of mine. He wasn't drinking because he knew he was going to drive," Steve recalls. "Well, after I kept him out too late, he fell asleep at the wheel, hit a parked car on the side of the road, and the car basically collapsed on us. The car was even on fire, but luckily my buddy had enough strength to pull me out of the car. I have pictures of this car after the accident; it was absolutely destroyed." After 2 weeks of hospitalization and a year filled with surgery and rehabilitation, Steve and his friend recovered.

Many people were surprised he'd lived. For instance, during his recovery at home, an insurance adjustor came to assess some damage at his parent's home. The adjustor saw his casts and started asking about the accident with a stunned expression on his face. "He said, 'I was the guy who appraised your car, and I was pretty sure that anyone in that car was dead,'" Steve recalls. Even though doctors told him he might never walk again, he recovered fully.

"That's what you call a 'wakeup call,'" Steve says. Even though he was only 19 years old, Steve started looking at his life and where he was going. "I decided I needed to focus and get done what I needed to get done." He switched schools and enrolled at Kansas State University, which didn't have a chapter of his fraternity. After a few months, he started a deejay business with some friends, playing music at sorority and fraternity parties. "We kind of mixed having fun and making money at the same time," he says. "That was my first opportunity to figure out business, though it was still more of a hobby at the time. I figured out how to get new business, how to sell."

At graduation from KSU, Steve at first figured he'd move to Chicago, one of his favorite cities. But by then he had gotten into the habit of stepping back and looking hard at his decisions. In reality, he

saw that Chicago would be fun, but it would be better to buckle down
and get a job at Sprint, the biggest employer in Kansas City, where he
hoped to learn discipline and training in a specialty.

His first job was in telemarketing sales where he cold-called small
businesses all day long. "It was good business experience," he says.
"You talk to a bunch of characters when you're doing this." Steve even
met one of his girlfriends through the telemarketing job, when he
talked to a young woman who was in Florida working as office manager for her father's electrician business. The job wasn't horrible, "but
it didn't feel like I was applying anything I'd learned in college," Steve
says.

Underestimating Obstacles

Before long, his contacts at Sprint landed him a job in billing at a
company that sold long distance service to nonprofit organizations.
The company was an affinity marketer; it sold long distance services
to nonprofit organizations, and a percentage of each paid bill went
back to the nonprofit. Most of the nonprofits the company worked
with were churches; telemarketers would play voice recordings from
each church's pastor, telling them how important it was for them to
sign up for this program so that their phone bills would help their
church raise funds.

His first business trip with this company was to a national religious broadcasters conference in Nashville. "Here I am, a back office
guy," recalls Steve, who is Jewish. "The group would go into a hotel
room before the day started, and they would pray together. I stayed
separate. After a while, I thought, 'Maybe this isn't the place for me.'"

Still, Steve felt he was learning some skills in billing, so he
switched to the competition. His new employer, Houston-based
Equalnet, also sold long distance services with a whole new level of

resources and energy. Here, Steve had a better atmosphere, a bigger title—Director of Billing—a bigger salary, and he learned everything there was to know about billing systems.

There were some challenges, though. First, he'd been hired from outside, so he had people on staff who were disappointed they hadn't received his job. Second, he didn't get any management training to prepare him for the job. "I knew the trade, but I didn't know how to manage people. I didn't understand leadership," Steve says. "Somebody would come into my office, they'd want to tell me an issue, they'd want to vent. I might be answering email and listening to them at the same time, not giving them my whole attention."

This is a pretty common problem. And Steve did what most people do: He muddled through as best he could. After all, no one was offering him any leadership either. "They were a bunch of young entrepreneurs. They didn't really focus much on management, but focused on getting business done," he recalls.

Eventually, Steve caught the eye of a headhunter. During the course of the phone interview, he figured out the company he was being recruited for was none other than Sprint PCS, a joint venture between some cable companies and Sprint. Steve saw that his strategy of learning a marketable skill had paid off. He jumped at the opportunity to work at Sprint PCS and moved back to Kansas City to be the head of his own group.

Building Momentum—Analytically

Now, at age 27, Steve's career at Sprint PCS took off with a bang. The company put him on a team where his first task was to speak at a board meeting and show evidence that the company should build a wholesale billing services group. Because that billing group would compete with the direct sales channel, it had some opposition. "We had a bit of time to justify why we ought to start wholesale," recalls Steve, who had a quick e-minute part in the conversation. "It was my first entreé to this c-level boardroom world. It was very cool."

Luckily, the board decided to grow the wholesale services group, and Steve grew it to a staff of over 30. "Since I'd managed two other billing groups, I knew what had to happen," he says. "We were our own small billing company within Sprint PCS."

Steve also began to attend classes for his MBA at the company's expense, and he learned how to give performance appraisals and how to lead people. He was even invited into the director development program at Sprint PCS. As part of that program, he acquired a mentor.

Here is where Steve stopped to analyze where he was going. He thought it was going pretty well until he asked his mentor for advice. His mentor told him to stop being a "subject matter expert" and focus on being someone who sees the big picture. Steve took his advice. "As a manager," he says, "I moved farther away from the technical track and more toward the soft side of how to motivate people, how to manage people, even when there were lots of layoffs and very little growth activity."

And his mentor told him something that surprised Steve: Get out of billing. If he got promoted in that track, he'd be stuck there forever. As Steve puts it, billing was "too niche and didn't really match my true passion, which was to be on the 'outside' dealing with customers face to face." If he ever wanted to move from Sprint or into a more dynamic role, his mentor advised, Steve must do it before he got a huge promotion in billing.

So Steve began a well-planned campaign to move into business development. This was nearly impossible because the company rarely moved people from operations to the more sought-after roles in business development. When he finally got an interview for a job in business development, Steve prepared by researching his interviewer. He found out the guy was very proud of his graduate degree from the University of Chicago. So Steve walked into his office and immediately commented on the diploma on the wall. "Oh, that's a fantastic school," he said. "After that, we really synched up well." The last step in the process was an interview with a vice president, who had come to Sprint from McKinsey & Co. So Steve dutifully read the book *The McKinsey Way*, a behind-the-scenes look at the consulting firm. From the book, he learned "these people at McKinsey always have three reasons for everything they do," Steve says. "I kind of slipped in some of the McKinsey-isms during the interview. And in my follow-up letter I wrote, 'Three reasons why you need to hire me.'" His extra effort paid off, and Steve got his foot in the door at business development.

"I got lots of good experience," says Steve, whose first challenge was to find a way to partner with Microsoft. Over a few years time, as he did more and more deals, he rose to senior manager of strategic business development. Steve was invited to speak at industry conferences. His star was rising.

Taking the Next Leap

Just when he was hitting his stride, Steve sat down and had another hard look at his options to plan and navigate his future. Even though he was out of billing and in business development, he was uneasy staying at Sprint PCS. He saw it would take ages for him to rise above the level of senior manager and into the higher ranks. "If there's any time that I want to leave, this is the time," he says. It was time to change course.

Steve started looking around for an emerging market where he could use his business development skills. One of the best places to look was at business conferences, which was where he met the Omnilink Systems people as they lined up to approach Sprint with a proposal for a business partnership. When Steve first met with the

Omnilink founder, he said, "You have 10 minutes. Tell me what you got." As the founder described the tracking product, Steve was interested—and not just on behalf of Sprint. When Steve asked the founder how he would put together a management team, he said the first hire would be the business development person. And, the founder added, "Let me know if you know anybody." Steve correctly took that as a hint of an invitation to join the startup. In that moment, he began to think about it.

Four months later, he jumped to Omnilink Systems. The startup, launched in 2003, is built around web-based software that can locate people wearing a monitoring device, whether they are indoors or outdoors. It's great for tracking paroled convicts or nonviolent criminals who are sentenced to home confinement but allowed to go to work each day. Omnilink's technology is even being used to keep track of Alzheimer's disease patients and to find lost pets.

Even though the bulk of Omnilink's customers are in law enforcement, part of Steve's job is to uncover the many uses for this technology. And he didn't burn any bridges at Sprint, which has actually become a strategic partner with Omnilink.

If Steve hadn't sat back several times over his career and charted a course, he might still be toiling for a promotion in a billing department somewhere. Lucky for him, he's in a stimulating job as a vice president; the first employee after the founders in a company that now has 43 employees and is still growing. In addition to a great salary, he has an ownership stake in a company that could pay off big someday. His story shows the power of taking control and charting your course. After all, it's more risky to close your eyes and ignore the direction in which you're heading, so go ahead and follow the stars.

What if Jumping to a Startup Doesn't Work Out?

One of my best friends recently had an opportunity to join an emerging consulting company that facilitated outsourcing work to China. It seemed like a fantastic opportunity, even though the company was small (just like when Steve made his jump). He asked me, "What if it doesn't work out?" My advice was to take it, be an early employee, and participate in the upside if the company grows. That was a little over a year ago. Fast forward to today: His company missed payroll for six weeks and couldn't reimburse him for an expensive business trip to China. The company crumbled due to a lack of cash flow and a large account not paying its bills on time.

Tragedy? I think not. Just like Randy Brandoff at Marquis Jet (Chapter 18, "Exercise Your Middle Brain"), my friend knew that the experience would be priceless, and he could always fall back into one of the larger consulting firms.

His experience learning the consulting business on an international level and traveling to China has made him even more valuable to the work place and/or more appealing to an MBA program if he ever wanted to go back and earn that degree.

As of today, after gathering his thoughts for a month or so, he found his dream job at an extremely exciting mid-sized company. He couldn't be happier with his new situation and would never have been qualified had he not taken the risk with the small outsourcing startup!

Financial Tip: Establish a career emergency fund. If you carry 3 to 6 months worth of reserve cash in a money market account, you have a reserve tank to fall back on if a calculated career move doesn't pay off. The more reserve you build up, the greater decision-making ability you will possess as you operate from a position of financial strength.

To subscribe to my monthly "Make More, Worry Less" newsletter, visit www.wesmoss.com.

Charting Your Own Course

It's crucial for us to take ownership of our careers and chart our own course. Steve walks us through the process with these simple steps:

- **Talk to yourself.** Ask yourself this hard question each day: How is what I did today going to get me where I want to be in my career? Be brutally honest with yourself!

- **Seek sage advice.** Periodically ask for advice from a mentor, an old college professor, or any other person you trust; find out whether they think your job is getting you where you want to go.

- **Analyze your options.** Read management books and business magazines, keep your ears open at business conferences, and look at what people are doing in other departments at your company.

- **Change course.** No one is ever 100 percent on course all the time. When necessary, pursue a job in a better field or department where you want to gain experience. Pull out all the stops to get you there, even if it means working for the competition or a smaller startup.

- **Navigate the waters.** Pay attention to your company's direction and the industry's business climate. If there are opportunities in your company, stay there. If not, go where the opportunities are.

If you would like to learn more about sharing the "Make More, Worry Less" message with your group or organization, visit www.wesmoss.com.

Wes's Worry Less Tip

► **Lucky to be here.**

So many times we do not recognize how lucky we are just to be alive; until we watch the 6:00 news and see someone shot one neighborhood away or see a mangled car along the highway that we just drove home on. This type of scare happens to all of us. We shouldn't need a life-threatening event, like Steve had, to realize how lucky we are. It's easy to get caught up in the importance of the next deal or the next raise or your next bonus. But like Steve, we're all lucky to be here. He gives thanks for his wife and family every day. No matter what could go wrong at work, we should all remember to appreciate what we do have.

"Only learn to seize good fortune, for good fortune is always here."

—Johann Wolfgang von Goethe

9

Command Attention

—Diana Ruddick (Leading Life Insurance Firm)

It's hard to get noticed. Even if you're hard-working and intelligent, managers don't always notice you. That's because managers are only human: They can overlook people who don't fit their picture of success. Diana Ruddick shows how you can command attention and work your way up the ladder, even if you're not what your boss considers to be leadership material. Diana's story isn't just for women: Men can learn from her because anyone can get stuck in a certain task or department where they are sidelined and never promoted. "It's easy to get classified as a 'process' person—someone who is *good at* something," says Diana, "but you have to go further and see the big picture." Her knack of seeing the big picture—and commanding the attention of her bosses—helped her advance through the ranks from insurance claims processor at a major health insurer to vice president of a leading life insurance carrier.

"I never got sucked into a really technical role," Diana says. "I had the opportunity to do this, but I didn't want to be cast as someone who was a process person. I found that leadership was a lot more fun."

However, at first, neither her bosses nor her coworkers saw her as someone who could be a leader. Diana's story isn't like Kevin Noland's (Chapter 6, "Be Distinct or Be Extinct"), who wowed people with his computer programming skills and enrolled in GE's management trainee program. Diana impressed people with her efficiency as a claims processor, but no one offered her a management trainee slot. And there were other obstacles: Coworkers disrespected her when she was supposed to supervise them, and one boss actually laughed when she asked for a promotion. But instead of letting them drag her down, Diana commanded their respect and ended up getting leadership roles—and doing very well at them.

What's so inspiring about Diana is that even though she had a few knocks early in her career, she kept at it and eventually changed people's opinions—and she didn't become bitter. Even though she wasn't offered her first opportunities, she pushed until she convinced people she could handle being a leader. Then, when she was recognized as a valuable go-to person, Diana worked to change her industry to make it easier for other women to command attention as well. Instead of souring her, those early knocks became Diana's inspiration to be the kind of leader who helps people better their job performance.

Starting from Scratch

Her first job, processing claims at a health insurer field office was just a way to bring in some extra cash when Diana was looking for a way to supplement her husband's income. After a few weeks on the job, she found there were a lot of jobs she could do at the health insurance company that she'd never dreamed of.

For instance, when Diana's supervisor quit, there was an opening for a claims processor to manage the unit. Several people had been there longer than Diana, but none of them wanted the job. So even though she was the low man, Diana went to the manager and asked to put her hat in the ring. "I figured he could tell me I'm not qualified or I could get the job," recalls Diana, who did get the job. But the promotion was a mixed blessing: Her former coworkers copped an attitude and ostracized her for her ambition. "It seemed like it took forever for these people to speak to me," Diana recalls.

Here's where Diana came upon her philosophy of leadership. She knew very well that the people she was supervising knew their jobs better than she did—they'd been there longer. And she understood their resentment. So she didn't bluff; instead, she admitted that they knew their jobs and commanded their attention with charming honesty and firmness. She sat down and said, "Look, here are the things that I can do for you as your leader. My job is to break down barriers, help you get what you want, help you get things done, help you solve problems that you think are insoluble. My job isn't to tell you how to do your job if I think you're doing it well."

And for good measure, Diana went to her boss and asked to have the person who continued to undermine her removed from the unit. Very assertive.

Diana led her unit as a problem-solver and learned a valuable lesson that she used throughout her career: It's more important for a manager to learn about leading people than to know the minutiae of a job. Her coworkers in the claims-processing unit, for instance, were good at their claims-processing jobs, but they didn't have the desire to be leaders—to be the ones to take responsibility and solve problems. Being a newbie was actually an advantage because Diana wasn't tempted to micromanage. "Often, what happens is the best technicians get promoted to where they're supervising others, but they still want to do things," Diana says. "So they're breathing down people's necks, not leaving them alone to do their jobs, not delegating. I have no problem letting people get their hands dirty. My job is to see the big picture."

While Diana scored a big victory in getting people to take her seriously, her battles weren't over.

Underestimating Obstacles

Next Diana heard of an opening for a claims investigator. Typically, the health insurer hired recent college graduates for the job and groomed them to manage claim offices. It sounded like a cool job. But when Diana told her boss she'd like to apply for the position, he laughed. "He didn't take me seriously and hired someone who knew nothing and expected me to train this guy," Diana recalls. "He said, 'It's not a job for women.'" So Diana marched to the EEOC (Equal Employment Opportunity Commission), the federal agency in charge of enforcing civil rights laws. She could have asked for reparations, such as back pay, but all she asked for was to be considered for the job. Diana ended up getting hired, and both she and the man who'd been hired were trained together. (Eventually, when another opening came up, the man moved and took that job.)

The job, it turned out, was fun. "It was interesting because I wasn't chained to a desk every day," Diana says. Her job was to interview people on disability to see if they truly had the injuries they claimed to have.

As she had hoped, that claims investigator job led to more responsibilities and promotions and landed her in the managed care unit of the insurance company's home office. But then her momentum slowed. That's because the managed care unit she'd worked so hard to get promoted into was a very price-sensitive business. And it was at the time when HMOs (health maintenance organizations) were replacing more traditional plans. So Diana found much of her job was about her taking the heat when employees found out what their insurance didn't cover. "It wasn't very rewarding," Diana recalls. "You climb the ladder of success and realize you're leaning against the wrong building."

Getting sidelined in an unexciting, low-growth part of the company is something that happens quite often to people. It might even be an obstacle you're facing right now or will face sometime in the future. If and when you find yourself sidelined, it's important to realize it's not the end of your career—it's just another obstacle to overcome.

That's how Diana looked at it. She continued doing a good job, continued commanding attention, and got noticed—this time outside of her company. A headhunter called and recruited her for a job at a smaller life insurance company. Even though she'd never heard of the new company, the new job represented a chance to get out of a rut. It just goes to show that if you make a name for yourself in one company—but your employer doesn't continue to challenge you with rewarding work—the solution might be to pack up and take your talents to a smaller company doing something slightly different.

Working at a smaller company, Diana had many opportunities to get noticed. For instance, at her first employer she'd been assigned to JCPenney's managed care program, which covered about 70,000 employees. At her new company, the group life and health business was trying to sign up employers with 100 employees or more. Diana knew how to help her new company get the business it wanted, and she dug into the job. After a time, she was running the group health and life unit at her new employer and traveled overseas to set up the company's Ireland subsidiary. Diana's skills got her noticed and promoted up to second vice president. And then something else came along.

Building Momentum—Helpfully

We all get comfortable in our jobs, yet Diana shows how rewarding it can be to accept change and new challenges. Working in the health insurance field had been her whole career. And her employer had given her opportunities to command attention across all its different business units. She'd sat on a leadership board with the man who ran the company's individual life insurance business. Out of the blue, he called and said, "Are you open to a different career opportunity?" Her new boss-to-be said her ability as a good leader and communicator was what he needed, and he wanted someone with a different perspective who would ask, "Why are we doing this?"

But the move had its risks. For one thing, Diana had never heard of anyone who jumped from health insurance to life insurance so late in their careers. Second of all, she wasn't sure she understood the life insurance business: "I didn't know anything about life insurance except that I had it." Still, the opportunity was attractive, so Diana jumped.

At first, Diana spent her time learning the business and the financial drivers behind the life insurance industry and learning what the problems were. A big part of her job was to be a liaison between the company and the independent agents who sold the company's life insurance. She got to know the agents, set up annual conferences for them to attend, and found a glaring omission: Very few women were selling life insurance.

The way she saw it, recruiting productive agents—men or women—is very important to the life insurance business, and not having many women agents meant that her employer was missing out on 50 percent of its possible recruits. Life insurance sales seemed like a wonderful business for women, who usually have great listening and problem-solving skills, Diana reasoned. So why weren't women attracted to this business?

She asked her employer for $250,000 to start various women's initiatives, and without many details, her boss gave it to her. By then she had a reputation as a problem-solver who makes things happen, and she didn't need to explain herself. Then she gathered up seven women to explore the barriers that kept women from getting into life insurance sales. She treated the group as an incubator for ideas, trying to break the code on this issue of the lack of women agents. It was a bold move.

And like many bold moves, it paid off. That first group became a women's advisory board that helped advise her employer on issues such as how the company appears to women, how to improve its marketing materials, and how to provide support to women agents. The program is still alive and well, and there are now 13 advisory boards throughout the country in markets that Diana hand-picks. These boards sponsor projects to improve financial literacy among women and girls in each community where they are active. They also act as mentors to women insurance agents.

Once a year, Diana and the chairs of the advisory boards get together and give the company feedback on its advertising and marketing materials. "They've become part of our company family, and they've become great friends of mine as well," Diana says. "I can call these women and say, 'Hey, I need a favor,' and they'll drop everything and help."

As she learned early in her career, helping others do their jobs is the best way to lead: "If you're going to survive and be effective in a large company, you have to help other people get what they want. Because sooner or later you're going to have to call on them to get what you want."

Taking the Next Leap

Diana loves where she is in her career, and it's not just because of the money. It's because she commands attention and respect. Not only does she have the eternal gratitude of her boss, she has something that money can't buy: "The real gratifying part is I have a reputation in the company. I've been here now long enough that I know a lot of people and I have a lot of influence. To me that's as important as anything."

For example, as vice president of communications, she has a seat at the table of the agent's association, which includes all the agents who sell her employer's insurance in the field. Although they're not technically employees, they need to know important information about the company's strategy—and they need to weigh in on it with their opinions. Once a year, Diana organizes a huge assembly of all the field agents, and it's something she looks forward to each year. "That's really the funnel through which we get intelligence, products of competitors, what customers want; it's really a way for us to keep our career agency system vibrant and healthy," she says. What happens in those groups is crucial to the future of the company, and Diana loves the work.

So far, the advisory boards that Diana set up have raised awareness and helped increase the number of women agents from 10 percent of the field force to 16 percent—and it's also helped build business for her employer. For example, a woman general agent in the D.C. area was trying to open markets for her agents in the area's small businesses and put together a video seminar to illustrate problem-solving for family-owned businesses. When the seminar was unveiled to the advisory board, one of the members was the CEO of the D.C. Chamber of Commerce. The CEO was so impressed with the seminar that she wanted it presented to her Chamber. "In one fell swoop, the general agent got access to the 3,000-member companies of the greater Washington, D.C. Chamber of Commerce, and not just women-owned business," Diana explains. "The ripple effect from these advisory boards is very great."

Diana has come a long way from her days as a claims processor who got the silent treatment from her staff, and she's never forgotten that her first job as a leader is to help people. Diana says she loves her job so much that someday she may "rewire" and cut down on her hours, but she could never see herself retiring. She loves having her finger on the company's pulse, and she loves putting together the annual agent meetings: "It's like having a party for 3,000 of my closest friends." When you push the envelope and command attention, the sky's the limit.

How to Command Attention

- Ask for responsibilities.
- Help people—your staff, coworkers, and boss—to solve their problems and do their jobs better.
- Call in your favors when you need help doing your job better.
- Be firm with people who undermine you: Either win them over or maneuver around them.
- As your reputation grows, use it wisely to continue fueling the success of your teams and yourself.

Wes's Worry Less Tip

► Home is home, work is work.

Worrying about work is inevitable—especially when we bring a pile of work home at night. And when we let our work worries and pressures into our homes, it just makes for more anxiety, which will affect the relationships with our children, our marriages, and our sleep—especially our sleep! As my uncle has always told me, "People who have troubled sleep, have troubled lives." For many years, Diana was one of those people who brought a bagful of work papers home with her nearly every night. The problem was, by the time she got home and had dinner she was out of the mood to open the bag. Then she felt more and more anxious and guilty because she would drag the bag home with the best intentions and not follow through! What did she do? She just stopped taking work home; except on rare occasions when she has no choice. It's very liberating, and it will help you have a good night's sleep. So if worries get you down and you're bringing work home too often, make a commitment to leave that work on your desk—stay late if you have to—but once you leave work go home and recharge.

*"Take rest; a field that has rested gives a
bountiful crop."*

—Ovid (43 BC–17 AD)

Part III
Notice Your Network

The next principle in the HUNT is "Notice your network," and it's a little different in the corporate setting than it is for entrepreneurs. But the similarities are important: In both the entrepreneurial and corporate worlds, informal relationships—not meetings and formal evaluations—are where the real business of business gets done. In both worlds, your network is your lifeblood. The difference when you work for someone else (versus running your own company) is that your network can get extremely complicated. After all, you've got your boss, your boss's boss, and your coworkers—and all those people are looking to get ahead, just like you are. But if you see other people in the company as obstacles you have to get over, you're likely to fail. The way to get ahead in a company is to walk the line between upsetting people and doing favors for them. You walk a fine line.

"You don't have to like someone to form an alliance at work," Jennifer Allyn (Chapter 5, "Rally for a Cause") told me. Jennifer, managing director for gender retention and advancement at PricewaterhouseCoopers, counsels people to have a broad group of "friends" at work—people who you do favors for and who can be counted on to do favors for you when you need them. It's not like your personal life where you're likely to have a small circle of trusted friends; a work network needs to be a big shallow lake, not a small deep pond.

Strong Alliances

Although everyone in this book has managed his or her network well, the people in Part III truly have excelled at it. Ralph Stayer found the key to his success was seeing the people below him as partners, not just workers. Ed Cortese sees the whole world as his network, and he remembers that whenever he walks out his front door. Isisara Bey manages a huge extended network of former colleagues and even stays in touch with her old college professors, who have helped her career several times. Greg Downey took a chance meeting with a professional athlete in a doctor's waiting room, and turned it into the foundation of his career. Everyone has his or her own style for building alliances; how do you build yours?

Be a Leader

When it comes to doing favors for people at work, don't forget the people under you: If your staff improves, you'll look great. In addition to meeting Linda Rabb (Chapter 1, "The Compound Income Effect"), I was also able to interview many of her coworkers and mentors. One of her early mentors is named David Cloud. When David moved up from sales agent to district coordinator, it was his first time supervising people. And his staff wasn't much—they were just about the lowest performing group of sales agents in his state of Georgia. He took these three part-time agents, sat them down, and promised them all a portion of his sales commissions over the next 3 months if they would come on board full-time. "I told them, 'I'm going to show you how to make this business work,'" he recalls. "It was the decision of whether to take care of my people and make sure they had a paycheck or write the business myself and make sure *I* had a paycheck. It was tough.

I chose to get them a paycheck." At the end of 3 months, all three of the agents chose to stay—and they helped make David's district the top producer in the state of Georgia by a wide margin. David continued to move up in the company, and now at age 32 he is earning close to a million dollars in commissions. Two heads—or three or fifty—are obviously better than one!

Even if you don't earn commissions, this philosophy of empowering the people you supervise is a good move. After all, if your staff learns to be self-motivating, you all get more done and become very valuable to your employer. Motivating and leading people is one of the most difficult skills to teach someone—much more difficult than the basics of a business. That's why it's important to remember to model the kind of behavior you want in return from the people under you as well as the people on your level and above.

Currency of Goodwill

One of the ways you build and sustain alliances is through the currency of goodwill. This is often called "office politics," and many times we think of that as something of which we'd rather not be a part. Instead of avoiding politics, learn how to play the game with integrity. It's very simple. Whenever you can, do something positive for your coworkers, bosses, and people below you; when you need a favor back, go ahead and ask. Avoid people who don't reciprocate. After all, playing politics doesn't mean playing the fool. You don't have to help people who don't return favors. The currency of goodwill can be like money in the bank—build it up, and you will have something to draw on when you take on a new project.

Have Mentors

Mentor relationships come in all shapes and sizes. As you read this book, ask yourself who your mentors have been and who you could ask to give you this kind of help. A boss can be a sort of mentor, but it's good to have mentors who aren't responsible for your compensation. Many companies have formal mentor programs you can enroll in; if not, consider approaching a retired executive. Make it a point to attend community groups such as Rotary, where these retirees can be found.

And if you have the chance, mentor others. What goes around, comes around. People who mentor others always say that when they teach someone else, they end up learning lessons as well.

Birds of a Feather

Another reason to manage your network is for the inner benefit. Your network will help you nurture your leadership, stamina, and commitment—all qualities you'll need to stay committed to your own success. The thing about corporate life is that even though you're surrounded by people, it can be a very lonely place. When you get turned down for a promotion or your pet project fails, who do you turn to? If you have a network of trusted people, you'll find a sympathetic ear; you'll know who the backstabbers are that you should avoid. And when those successes come, you'll have people to help you uncork the champagne.

Instead of moaning about how the corporate world is filled with mediocre people—and it is—build yourself a network of go-getters like yourself. After all, doctors know other doctors, lawyers know lawyers, and movers and shakers know other movers and shakers.

When you feel surrounded by laggards, go find your flock of successful birds. After all, birds of a feather flock together.

Your network is your career's infrastructure—the roads and bridges that will move you along your career path. The stories in the next few chapters have some great lessons about how to build your network.

Hallmarks of People Who Notice Their Network

Building a solid network within your company is extraordinarily important for your career. It's the equivalent to the entrepreneur finding the right employees to help a burgeoning company grow. How do people really "Notice their network?"

- They create strong alliances.
- They are leaders, not managers. (Whenever you supervise others, you should strive to empower them rather than micromanage them.)
- They bank a currency of goodwill. (When was the last time you did a favor for someone at work? Return favors and avoid people who don't return them.)
- They have mentors. (You should have different mentors, both formal and informal, for different parts of your life.)
- They keep a small group of trusted confidantes.

Wes's Worry Less Tip

► Let go of blame and revenge.

Maybe it's human nature to blame others and wish for revenge; we've all wanted a big oak tree to fall on our neighbor's house at one time or another. But in reality, blame and revenge take too much time and energy; it's just not worth it. Vengeance and blame are first cousins to worry. There's always going to be people and circumstances to blame; but nothing matters less. How can you help your situation by blaming someone else? What matters is your ability to solve the problem. Blame and vengeful thoughts are not only a waste of time, psychologists say they're even damaging to our health. Revenge is a mental black hole, and I can't think of a bigger waste of time!

My advice—don't worry about who's to blame or how to get even; the answers to your problems always lie ahead, questions as to why you are in the position that you are in, are always a thing of the past. Choose to move forward and focus on the answers. I don't need questions about why it happened; I need answers on how to fix it! If your plane is late, it's not going to do any good to be angry with the pilot or the airline or the flight attendant. If you follow through with your vengeful thoughts, you're going to look like a fool when you get carried off by the FAA. The question is not "Why is my flight delayed" (because it already is), but "How can I find another flight?" If I'm going to be delayed, sitting around the airport, then what can I do with my time? So read a magazine, answer your email, or take a nap in the airport. Let go of the problem and embrace the solution.

"A man doesn't have the time to spend half his life in quarrels. If any man ceases to attack me, I never remember the past against him."

—Abraham Lincoln

For more about how Wes can help members of your organization "Notice Their Network," visit www.wesmoss.com.

For more Worry Less Tips, visist www.wesmoss.com.

10

The Butterfly Effect

—Ralph Stayer (Johnsonville Sausage)

Listen to that sick feeling in your gut. Most of the time we try to avoid that nervous butterflies-in-the-stomach feeling. But Ralph Stayer owes his career success—and the success of the hundreds of employees he supervises—to going after that butterfly feeling.

"If the things you commit to don't make you puke in the sink every now and then, you really haven't signed on for a lot," says Ralph, in his booming voice and plain Midwestern accent. His point is that it's important to look inside at the things we're afraid of and then go ahead and tackle 'em. That's how he built his career at Johnsonville Sausage.

Ralph's career started in one of the most comfortable, protected situations: a family business. It might have been easy for him to glide along and not push himself. Many people are in his situation today: Two out of five Fortune 500 firms are family businesses. And most American companies are run by brothers and sisters, mothers and fathers. So I include Ralph's story in this book because obviously a lot of people are working in businesses owned by their families. And even if you aren't, Ralph's story can apply to most situations, family business or not—because it's about how to manage people and improve yourself.

I really relate to Ralph's story because I got my start through family—and, like him, I couldn't sit back and glide. My uncle talked me into joining his profession as a financial advisor, and I started out at Prudential, the company where he worked. But, thankfully, my uncle made it clear to me that he was scaling back and didn't have any positions for me on his team. Because I knew I couldn't rest on my laurels and count on any more help from him, I had to make things happen for myself. Later, when I did find success operating on my own, my uncle asked me to join his team—it was then that I knew I'd made it.

So family business can give people a great start, but they don't guarantee success; that comes when people push themselves into the gut-wrenching zone. For Ralph, the pushing began in college, when he was studying business and finance at Notre Dame. Ralph worked out things on paper and saw that the retail sausage business wasn't going to make his family wealthy. Annual sales were about $1 million, and the three shops were profitable. But no matter how much he brainstormed, he couldn't see how to make the sausage shops into a big, growing concern. Somehow, though, he knew he would find an answer.

Starting from Scratch

The thought that he might not be able to help his parents grow their business gave Ralph a pretty sick feeling. After all, his parents had started the sausage shop in 1945, worked their way out of the poverty of the Great Depression through the sausage business, and sent Ralph to college in the hopes that he could help them grow the business. So he came up with something daring: create a wholesale manufacturing side of the business, which meant stepping up production, buying delivery trucks, and hiring more workers. It was a pretty big goal, but he couldn't let himself aim for anything less.

So instead of just getting by in a comfy family job, Ralph asked his parents to let him create a position for himself where he would grow the wholesale side of the sausage business. Of course, they said yes.

Making sausage, Ralph says, "is not rocket science." But keeping the product quality consistent with a proud family recipe is a daily battle. Or at least it was for him. So he tasted each day's batch of sausage and gave the workers feedback. Sometimes it was perfect, sometimes too spicy, other times the quality of the meat might not be the best. Ralph worked hard on every detail of sausage making, selling, finance, and distribution—and it paid off.

In 10 years, Ralph had a profitable wholesale business, and his parents made him president of the entire organization. That was in 1978, the same year the company broke ground on a new production facility and started moving its sausage beyond Wisconsin and into neighboring states. Sales were growing at double-digit rates each year, and Johnsonville Sausage wasn't a small, local producer anymore. It was a leading regional sausage supplier. Ralph should have been happy.

But the most interesting part about Ralph's story isn't his early success; it's how he didn't crash and burn. Because early on, Ralph listened to his gut: He knew Johnsonville Sausage was a vulnerable company.

Underestimating Obstacles

Here's the thing about problems: If you know they're there, you can solve them. If you deny them, they'll trip you up. Ralph listened to his gut: Underneath the success lurked a huge problem. Despite strong sales and profitability, Johnsonville Sausage was too large to be considered a small local brand (the kind that inspires strong community loyalty) and not big enough to compete with the large nationals like Armour Star and Oscar Mayer. Ralph needed to push and grow the company further, but that gave him the butterflies-in-his-stomach feeling—so he did it.

Whether you're making sausage or doing financial planning, growth has its problems. The problem with growth, in almost any kind of business, is that as more and more people take part in the business, it's harder to control the quality of the product. Ralph's problem was that Johnsonville must grow—or else be targeted by national brands with more money to spend on advertising and marketing—but in order to grow, quality control had to improve.

"I realized I couldn't keep on doing what I was doing," Ralph recalls. Even though he was working more and more hours, "We were making more and more mistakes. People didn't really care. They came, and they went. I tried every management recipe there was." Ralph was·reading management books as well as hiring consultants to study this and study that. Nothing was working. "I tried a bunch of stuff," he says. "It was all about *me* trying to fix *them*."

Then he went to a business event and heard a speech by Lee Thayer, a University of Wisconsin consultant. Something about Thayer's common-sense talk made Ralph think he could help him with Johnsonville's quality-control issue. But when Ralph asked the consultant to work for him, he got this answer: "It depends on what part of the problem you think *you* are." Dumbfounded, Ralph felt like he'd been hit in the gut: The consultant was saying that he himself was the problem. After Ralph regained his composure, he saw the opportunity. "I said, 'That's great because if I'm the problem, then I have the solution. I can fix me.'"

Building Momentum—Accountably

First, Ralph sent a six-page letter to each of his employees—along with a $200 check. In the letter, he explained how Johnsonville's workers could be the best-paid of the industry if the company continued to grow. And furthermore, employees would no longer be considered employees or workers, but referred to as "members," members of the Johnsonville team. But they needed to figure out how to make the plant run better. Maybe the process would be a little chaotic, maybe some people thought it was pointless; no matter, Ralph was boldly going into new management territory. What gave him the courage? It made sense. For years, he'd been the center of the business: "I was everything back then, in my own mind. My people deferred to me. The more I did, of course, the less they did."

Everything had to change, even the daily sausage-tasting where Ralph and two vice presidents graded the previous day's product and told the workers what they thought. As they stood there chewing, Ralph looked over at his vice president of manufacturing and said, "Did you make any of this sausage?" The vice president answered, through a mouthful of sausage, "No, of course not. I was in a meeting with you all day." Ralph stood there chewing and said, "I didn't make any of this stuff either. Why are we tasting the sausage?" The production workers, he realized, were responsible for making the sausage, so they should be tasting it. "We went running down to the factory and told them, 'From now on, you guys taste the sausage.'" Instead of feeling empowered, the workers' response was, "How will *we* know if it's any good?" Ralph felt horrible when he saw how little confidence the workers had in themselves. Empowering his "members" and making them accountable, he saw, was the real solution to helping Johnsonville grow.

After spelling out parameters for what makes great sausage— coming up with a scale for juiciness, tenderness, flavor, and texture— Ralph handed over tasting duties to the employees. But things didn't turn out exactly as Ralph expected. The sausage didn't just become more uniform—the sausage actually improved to be better than it used to be. How did that happen? Because the workers could see the cause and effect, such as which smokehouses supplied the best meat or where to get the best spices.

For years Ralph been working hard and using all his learning and resources to grow Johnsonville. But he'd forgotten about the learning and resources of his employees. Here they were, responsible people who could take care of themselves and their families, balance their checkbooks, and coach their children's Little League teams. But he was not giving them the chance to be accountable and use their talents.

More and more responsibility was delegated from managers to line workers. For instance, when employees complained about the food in the vending machines, they were given a chance to research and find a better supplier. And when production workers resented working weekends, Ralph gave them the task of figuring out how to increase efficiency and reduce waste during weekdays so they could shut down the factory on weekends. The first changes were on the production end, but it gradually extended to every department, with "members" taking over everything from marketing campaigns to merchandising programs.

Certainly expensive mistakes did—and do—happen at Johnsonville because the greater the accountability of employees, the greater the risk. But instead of focusing on someone's failure, Ralph says, "I prize the learning." He sees the expense of losses as the cost of investment in the employee's training. If you let someone go every time he or she makes a mistake, "you lose the investment."

Johnsonville was becoming a pretty unusual place. Workers became "team members," managers became "mentors," and benefits (which sound like manna from heaven) became "compensation." Changes came fast and furious; some people didn't like it and left. But there was no turning back for Ralph, who was excited again about coming to work each day.

Taking the Next Leap

Ralph isn't surprised that his experiment worked, but the numbers are amazing. Between 1980 and 1985, the company became more efficient and raised its return on assets. Sales climbed to

$50 million by 1985, up from $15 million in 1982. Now sales are more than $600 million, and more than a third of net pretax profit now goes out in bonuses to the "members." Even with all that bonus money paid out, net profit on sales has *tripled*.

"We make a lot of money, one of the most profitable businesses in our industry. But profits aren't about money alone," Ralph says. "It's about people." If the company has a year when it doesn't grow by at least 15 percent, Ralph and his people take it as a sign that they're stagnating. "It gets us back on track."

All this focus on challenging himself—and his employees—means Ralph sees his career differently than when he first set out to build a wholesale manufacturing company. Instead of being the brains of the operation, as he used to see himself, now he sees himself as a coach and mentor. Instead of figuring out how to make more money, he says his job is "to figure out how to be the leader of the best sausage company in the world."

That means offering plenty of coaching and career help to employees. "What's the stretch? What gives you butterflies in your gut?" Ralph asks his managers. "Results are secondary; it's about producing great people."

Everyone's goals are now posted on the company's intranet. "Everyone sees it," Ralph says. "You can't hide." For a factory worker newly arrived to the United States, the goal might be to become fluent in English within 2 years; for a manager the goal could be to become a nationally recognized expert and be a paid speaker on that topic. And Ralph's goal? "To become a better leader."

Even more interesting is how the company goal, to become the best sausage company in the country, has changed. Now that Johnsonville is an industry leader, "it's not a stretch anymore" to be the best sausage company. So the Johnsonville "members" got together and changed the goal. Now it's to become the country's best company—of any kind. The old goal just wasn't causing enough butterflies in the stomach.

Whenever I get butterflies in my stomach at the thought of taking a risk—doing my own radio show, talking about my work on television, or coming up with a new book proposal—I push myself through it, and then I'm glad I did. Now that I've met Ralph and heard his story, I'll think of how he started as an employee working for his parents and then buit Johnsonville Sausage into a huge company that he now heads. Even though most of us may not enjoy that uncomfortable, fluttery feeling in our stomachs, Ralph's story can help us to see it as a precursor to great things.

> *"Nerves and butterflies are fine—they're a physical sign that you're mentally ready and eager. You have to get the butterflies to fly in formation; that's the trick."*
> —Steve Bull

And Ralph has a great philosophy for managing people: "I was lying awake nights trying to figure out how to make great quality sausage. That's not my job. My job is to lie awake nights coming up with ways to get the people who are making the sausage to lie awake nights thinking about how to make great quality sausage."

Whether you manage people now or will in the future, think of Ralph when you tackle a big goal. And if you feel butterflies, you may be on to something great!

Butterfly in the Making

There are five steps for pushing yourself beyond your comfort zone into the zone where you get that butterflies-in-the-stomach feeling. It works for Ralph Stayer and his employees—try it for yourself.

1. Sit down with a trusted mentor and figure out what goal would be a huge stretch for you.

2. Post the list of achievements where you will see them each day.

3. Whenever you make a mistake, admit responsibility and learn how you could do better next time.

4. Meet each month with your mentor to see where you stand.

5. When you reach the goal, set the bar higher and start over!

Wes's Worry Less Tip

▶ **Move forward.**

Second guessing is the root of so much worry. We think: If we hadn't done this or hadn't done that, we wouldn't be here today. I say second guessing is useless. Sure we want to learn from the past, but most of the time it doesn't matter. You're in the situation that you're in, and that's the important issue to solve. If you're constantly looking over your shoulder about why you're in the position you're in today, then you're spending less time solving today's issue. Today's issue is what matters, not yesterday's. Looking over your shoulder equals worry; keep your attention on today's solution.

"The past is a nice place to visit, but I wouldn't want to live there."

—Anonymous

To contact Wes about putting more butterflies into your company's mix, visit www.wesmoss.com.

11

Look the Part

—Ed Cortese (Robb Report)

In his many marketing jobs, Ed Cortese learned to think of himself as the head executive of "Ed Cortese Inc." and to make sure he looked the part every day. No matter what hat he wore at work—and we all wear a lot of different hats at our jobs these days—he looked like George Clooney on the set of *Ocean's 11*—relaxed and quietly confident. Ed shows that looking the part is more a state of mind than a style of dress.

"Operate your career as if you're your own little company and you've been contracted to do the work," Ed says. "Stand up with your back straight, with a big smile, and be proud of who you are."

Ed's philosophy helped him get his foot in the door of New York's fashion marketing world right out of college, but you don't have to be in the fashion industry to use his advice. The main thing is to use your physical image to project that you have the smarts and the confidence to get the job done—whatever that job might be. On an average day, Ed might wear a dark suit and white shirt when he's in the office all day, but he brings a blazer and loafers to switch into if he has to have lunch with a client in a more relaxed setting. Whatever outfit he wears, Ed says he uses his posture and his whole demeanor as a tool to communicate the message that he's competent and valuable. And that's not all: Ed always has a quick elevator speech in his head to introduce himself to people he bumps into each day. After all, he's representing himself and his employer—and you never know who's watching.

It may seem unfair that we're judged by our appearance, but then again who would you rather trust with your life savings—someone well dressed with a crisp, clean dark suit, or a slouch with green tweed trousers that don't fit and socks that don't match? Well, if appearance doesn't matter, and something superficial such as clothing shouldn't matter, then consider this notion from the famous Lawrence Bell (founder of Bell Aircraft Corporation and considered to be the dean of American aviation in the 1950s):

> *Show me a man who cannot bother to do little things, and I'll show you a man who cannot be trusted to do big things.*

We all want to get the most for our money, and employers are no different; they want that payroll to buy the best value possible for their company. I'm not saying that being well-groomed will help you get ahead if you don't also have what it takes to do the job. But there's a lot of competition out there, and *not* looking the part can sabotage all your capabilities and hard work. Ed's attention to the details of his appearance kept him getting noticed as he climbed his career ladder—in prosperous times as well as lean times. Now he's in his dream job as marketing director for *Robb Report*, a magazine about the luxury lifestyle.

The story of how he got to the director position will get you thinking about your own image. Because we all need to wear a lot of different hats at our jobs, it's important to sit back and look at the image we project. Your image should always remind people that one of the hats you wear is captain of your own ship. As you move up to the top of the ladder, you'll see that the rungs get narrower; there's room for fewer people the closer you get to the top. Just being good at your job isn't always enough. Ed saw that and used his image—as well as his good sense and experience—to do good work and get noticed.

Early on, he saw that it wasn't enough just to be competent and hard working; he had to *look* competent and hard working. He had to learn to look the part.

Starting from Scratch

Ed got into marketing because it was what he knew. "I grew up hearing about it. It was a natural for me," says Ed, whose father worked in the marketing field. So Ed majored in business at New York University, focusing on public relations and marketing. That's how a lot of us find our careers—through family influences. And there's nothing wrong with that.

Growing up on Long Island, Ed loved New York City, and he also loved to travel. His parents took family trips to far-flung locations, so he was exposed to culture at an early age. In high school he loved to spend the day walking around the Metropolitan Museum of Art or Greenwich Village and then come home at the end of the day on the train. "I guess I had a sense and awareness of style," Ed says. So his understanding of style was his natural love.

When he graduated from college, Ed started working for his father a bit and looking for a real job. That's when a he found an "in" through a neighbor who sold ads for *GQ* magazine, a men's lifestyle publication. She told him of an opening at the magazine he should apply for. So he did, and Ed ended up getting called in for an interview. The interview ended up being very casual—they talked about their favorite restaurants in Los Angeles and the latest celebrity gossip, such as the fact that Richard Gere apparently employed a numerologist. "We just talked about all these random things," Ed says. "It didn't seem like an interview at all. When I left I thought, 'What was that?'"

It ended up being a very good sign. *GQ* called in Ed for five more interviews as well as a camera test. Then one day at 7 a.m. they called and asked if he'd like the job, which was as a merchandising editor. Ed jumped at the chance. He would represent the magazine at media events *GQ* held at department stores. Ed would pull clothing from the racks for the models and make sure the message of the event matched the message *GQ* wanted to project. He was thrilled.

Ed's proximity to New York's fashion industry was his natural edge; his sense of style was his natural love. Bringing the two together to make a career in the fashion industry made sense.

The job wasn't just about style—Ed was there to get results for his employer. So he started to run the numbers and figure which kind of events brought in the most business for the magazine. Also he started writing articles for *GQ*'s newsletter, which was circulated to its advertisers, thinking it would help drum up more advertising revenue. Ed worked at *GQ* from 1988 to 1994 and loved it. Leaving there was unplanned, but it seemed like a good idea at the time.

The next opportunity was a detour. Ed would still be working in the fashion industry, but he would try something new: on-air host of Q2 Television, an upscale home shopping channel. Q2, which was a startup owned by QVC, was an adventure. Some of the other on-air hosts had talent agents and came from the modeling world. Ed didn't. He was hired more for his knowledge of the fashion industry. Standing up in front of a camera hawking luxury items, Ed saw the power of image.

"You have to always be aware of the first impression," Ed says. "You're perceived as the front line of your company, and it's not just in public relations and advertising. This is true in all lines of work."

So even if we're not literally up in front of a camera in our jobs, we might as well be. That's because people are so influenced by what they see in front of them. Instead of throwing up our hands about it, we can be like Ed and make it work for us.

"The way you dress is a kind of communication," he says. "You send a message with your attire."

Underestimating Obstacles

Unfortunately, the new network didn't take off. "The products were too upscale for its audience," Ed says. "Home shopping had not yet taken off." After Q2, Ed's career was a string of fashion industry jobs that he did well in, but didn't feel exactly right.

First there was the job at *Harper's Bazaar*, where he did some of the same kinds of things he'd done at *GQ*. Next he moved to Nine West Group, which designs and markets women's shoes, where he was starting to have some creative control over marketing strategy. After that he took a bit of a sidestep at Ralph Lauren Footwear, which wasn't all it was cracked up to be. "The job was sold to me as if I'd have some creative involvement," Ed says, "but that was an enormous exaggeration. Maybe I was just starry eyed to be back in New York, working with the Ralph Lauren brand." Whatever the case, Ed chalked it up as a lesson. He should have researched the job better, he says now.

After a short stint at Ralph Lauren, Ed put out his own shingle and set up his own public relations company—with mixed results. "I found the spirit of entrepreneurship is very difficult to execute in real life," says Ed, who found it overwhelming to run a startup. Even though he was used to wearing a lot of hats, he didn't have time to do the business end of things—such as collecting on accounts—and didn't have enough cash to hire someone to do it. Plus, he missed working with a team.

It's one thing to underestimate obstacles, but it's foolhardy to ignore reality. And the reality was that running his own PR firm really wasn't what Ed wanted to do. So he worked his connections and again started looking for another job.

The next stage of Ed's career was marked by the technology boom and bust.

It started with a job at MAGIC International, which hosts a huge event every year to bring together buyers and sellers in the apparel industry. Ed's job was to head up MAGIC's fledgling dot-com project, which was to be an online center for business-to-business commerce in the apparel industry. "I was really excited about that," Ed recalls. "Two years we plugged away at that, and for a bunch of reasons the final online product did not work. The actual software didn't work. It was disastrous." When the project began to implode, the employees were called together in a conference and told what was going on.

"You're in this industry that's exploding, all you hear is dot-com, dot-com, dot-com...and before you know, it's dot-*gone*," Ed recalls. This was a tough time, but Ed managed to stay upbeat.

Building Momentum—Confidently

Luckily, the job at MAGIC led to a job at WGSN.com, one of MAGIC's online partners that had a working site with industry information about trade shows, designers, and fashion editors. His boss at MAGIC recommended him, and Ed was grateful. To this day, he thinks it was because he knew how to project a successful image for WGSN.

At first, WGSN seemed like a dream job. Ed spent his days in the showrooms of designers, such as Hilfiger, Levi's, and Saks Fifth Avenue. He was in charge of cultivating connections that were vital to the website, and he loved it. Then his employer invested in technology that would let Ed communicate online with his fashion contacts instead of in person—it was supposed to boost productivity. Instead of establishing relationships in person, he was chatting online, and Ed was all about that person-to-person touch. "It didn't matter what I wore; I could be in pajamas at home," Ed recalls. "It took the wind out of my sails. Even though this was something I was great at, they could tell I wasn't happy. They were paying me a lot of money for my selling and connections." So Ed negotiated a separation agreement and took some time off.

Although he still hadn't found his dream job, Ed had done well. He had money in the bank, he owned a home, and he was prudent about money. "I think it's really important to protect yourself financially in this world," Ed says. With a financial cushion, the lean times didn't hurt as bad. As a kid he'd mown lawns and saved up enough to help make a down-payment on a New York apartment early on in his career. When he sold the apartment, he was able to get a great home in suburban Long Island. So Ed planned his next move.

Besides cultivating financial health, it's wise to cultivate our spiritual and psychological health. This is something very personal that a lot of folks are a little shy to talk about, but Ed shared with me how he used prayer to get himself through this part in his life. One of his old college friends was marketing director at the *Robb Report,* a job that Ed wanted. "So I prayed that Bill would be offered a job that he couldn't refuse," and create a job opening, says Ed, who's a little sheepish about this part of his story because he doesn't want to sound like a religious fanatic. "I decided I didn't want to pray for my benefit directly." And, yes, it happened. Bill got an even better job, recommended Ed for the vacated position, and he was hired.

I include this story because it shows such strength of character— and I love that. Instead of drowning in envy that his friend had the job he wanted, Ed used prayer to stay constructive and positive. Instead of praying for his own enrichment, Ed prayed for his friend's benefit. Getting the job, after all, was up to Ed's own effort, not divine intervention. And when the call came for an interview at *Robb Report,* Ed was in a positive, vibrant frame of mind. His image wasn't just skin deep—he truly felt confident and valuable.

Taking the Next Leap

When Ed joined *Robb Report* in 2003, it was a little-known magazine; now it's at the forefront of luxury media. Although he knows it's not all his doing—an acquisition by CurtCo Media pumped cash into the brand—Ed has successfully drawn on his industry experience to grow the magazine and its visibility. Thanks to his experience running events earlier in his career, Ed used the magazine's annual "Best of the Best" issue to stage huge annual events showcasing luxury watchmakers, jewelers, and makers of other luxury items.

Before Ed joined *Robb Report,* the magazine had staged a regional "Best of Greenwich" event, but Ed decided to "blow those events out" and make them the backbone of *Robb Report*'s marketing. "At our events we try to bring each brand to life. It's not about having the Rolls Royce there; we have the president of Rolls Royce there and one of the senior engineers," Ed says. "It's not just about having jewelry there. It's about having the stonecutter there with his table, actually cutting the stone or setting the gem so you can really be part of it."

Instead of having the events in one area of the country, Ed located pockets of wealth throughout the country and hosted events in those communities. "By making an impact in one of these communities, we're able to create a big buzz," he says. And the events span 3 days, including a private dinner, a golf invitational tournament, as well as the main event.

Ed is still using what he has learned about projecting the right image: "When I'm in New York I wear a suit, shirt, tie—it's pretty buttoned up. If I do site inspections in Greenwich for an event, I don't want to walk around in a gray pinstripe suit—all of a sudden I look like a lawyer. So I'm going to put on an oxford, chinos, navy blazer, loafers, and I'm just going to slip into the community. I can be a chameleon."

Looking the part is only half the story, of course—you need to have some substance to back up your image. But if you use your image skillfully, use it as a way to make people feel comfortable and confident in you, more power to you. "There are tools you can use to enhance your business and make things easier, more comfortable. You just have to be smart about it."

Recently, Ed was in Monte Carlo for a *Robb* event, standing on a 285-foot yacht in his stocking feet (because it's good form to remove your shoes when you walk on someone's yacht.) There he was, standing between a billionaire and a waiter who was serving them drinks, and Ed looked down to see they were all three wearing Gold Toe brand socks, a good quality, affordable sock brand. It helped remind him that waiters and billionaires can all appreciate good, everyday quality—and that good quality doesn't have to be out-of-sight expensive.

In the same line of thinking, having a good image doesn't have to break your bank or turn you into a shallow person. After all, if you believe in yourself, then why not pay attention to the packaging on the outside?

Looks aren't everything, but the way we look communicates a lot about us. If you're an 'entrepreneur undercover,' you're thinking about your career as your own personal business, so you have to look the part. This goes way beyond "dressing for success" in the traditional sense of wearing a nice suit. In addition to picking up the skills you need, your reflection in the mirror should say you're someone who can create value.

How to Look the Part

I've never known a really successful business executive who didn't know how to look sharp. Physical appearance isn't everything, but it's a baseline that we should master. We don't all have to wear custom-made suits, but there's no excuse not to have a few classic power suits in your closet. Ed has these three tips that everyone should keep in mind.

- **Look in the mirror.** Do you project an image that matches your ability and goals?
- **Be a chameleon.** Dress nicely but not stiff. You want your image to help people around you feel comfortable and relaxed.
- **Exude confidence.** This goes deeper than clothing and includes your posture and overall attitude.

Wes's Worry Less Tip

- ## Focus on the power of one step.

    Whenever he's feeling overwhelmed and worried, Ed reminds himself that he's one guy taking one step. He says it makes him worry less because instead of looking at a task as an insurmountable journey, he focuses on one or two things he knows he can get done today. Instead of saying: "What can I do? I'm just one person with one rake in one hour...I can't possibly rake all the leaves in the yard!" He says: "Look at how much I can do right now!" When we see the power of putting one foot in front of the other and working steadily, projects seems less daunting. Small steps can lead to grand results. We need to be happy with our next step and see the power in accomplishing it.

*"Even a journey of a thousand miles begins
with one step."*

—Lao-Tzu

12

Walk a Mile in Their Shoes

—Isisara Bey (Sony BMG Music Entertainment)

It's probably one of the oldest proverbs around, and it's so true: Walking a mile in someone else's shoes—being empathetic—is important for a happy and successful life. That's right. Empathy isn't just some nice frosting on the cake; it's a very powerful trait—in your career and in the workplace. I'm convinced of this after speaking with Isisara Bey about her 20-plus-year career in the media and entertainment industry. She found that seeing other people's points of view—whether it's her boss, her colleagues, or members of Congress—earned her respect and the powerful position of vice president of corporate affairs at Sony BMG Music Entertainment.

Now, we usually think of empathy as a soft, squishy, intangible trait that makes for good friendships, but not exactly a great career mover. Wrong, says Isisara. For one thing, if you tend to see other people's points of view and respond to their concerns, they will "follow you to the ends of the earth," Isisara says. This might all sound pie in the sky, except Isisara is realistic and notes that you don't have to convince the whole company to see your point of view. "All you really need is one person who trusts you enough to say, 'Go ahead and do it.'"

For example, at a key moment in her career, Isisara's boss gave her 10 months to prove that she could handle a promotion. That's rough. She could have felt hurt and angry at her boss's lack of confidence, but Isisara's empathy helped her see it through her boss's eyes: She was young, less experienced than the person she was replacing, and the post was extremely important. She realized that her boss was just voicing his fear of what could happen to the company if she failed. So instead of getting bogged down in hurt feelings, Isisara came up with a plan to prove his fears were wrong.

In a three-step process, Isisara got busy. First, she asked her boss to assign her an executive coach to help her adjust to the promotion. Second, she asked for help from one person in the company whose respect she'd earned—he was in a different department, but he was powerful and used his influence to help her get nominated as a member of an important board. Third, she brainstormed, came up with some great new ideas to make her mark, and carried it all off— within the 10-month trial period. When her boss acknowledged she was off probation, it was a huge boost for her ego *and* her career.

Isisara doesn't just use empathy in her own career; she's made it part of her job to educate executives at Sony BMG about how to use empathy as a leadership tool. For instance, if executives empathize with employees, they see that many workers are ruled by fear—of losing their jobs, losing promotions, or losing prestige. And fear isn't a great way to manage people. Instead, she works to encourage a more empathic corporate culture where executives communicate goals with employees—who are then more efficient and focused. "Employees will take budget cuts and cutbacks in resources if they know they are part of a team," Isisara says. "If executives don't communicate, don't hang out in the cafeteria, don't call folks together, what they get are fearful, disgruntled employees."

Seeing the world through different perspectives came naturally to Isisara, maybe because she saw the world through two different cultures. She was born in New York, but her parents were immigrants from Guyana, and they took her to South America several times during her childhood. But even if we don't have her multicultural experience, we can all learn to have some empathy, Isisara believes, and a little can go a long way. Her story shows us how learning to walk a mile in someone else's shoes can be a powerful thing that fuels the corporate bottom line—and your own career.

Starting from Scratch

During college, Isisara had a few false starts. She was grieving over her mother's death, and part of her wanted to skip college and run back to Guyana to find a sense of security. But realistically, she saw that in a struggling, young country like Guyana, an unskilled young person wasn't going to get very far or be much help. So she stayed in the U.S. and majored in theatre, her first love. At graduation, she didn't think she had what it took to be an actress. Instead, she went to graduate school for a master's degree in media communications; as part of her studies at Antioch University, she ended up working at the Morgan University public radio station. The station was a National Public Radio affiliate in Baltimore, so her job as a morning drive radio personality was prestigious (and low-paying). She was finding her groove.

Her radio job brought back memories of Guyana and how important radio was to that developing nation when she visited as a child. "They didn't always have newspapers or televisions; the radio provided everything," Isisara recalls. One of her childhood memories is of walking with her mother through the streets of Georgetown, the capital of Guyana, rushing home to hear that night's radio show. "We didn't miss anything," Isisara says. "Because from block to block everyone was listening to the same thing. The radio shows had news, sports, class instruction, and death announcements for Guyanese anywhere in the world. I really began to love radio and how it would impact the imagination and connect people."

Already, Isisara's empathy made her love her work for the benefits it brought to people. And that's an important thing in corporate

America—it will keep you fired up about your career. After all, most of the day-to-day work in corporations isn't flashy and fun; there are always some boring daily tasks. But if you love the *benefits* your work brings to the world, it'll keep you sharp. For instance, I may not always love each and every task or five-hour meeting that is required of me to be a successful financial planner, but I can love the results it brings to people: financial and emotional security. You can do this with almost any job, and it will help keep you working at your best.

For instance, in Isisara's job as radio personality, she was on air from 6 a.m. to 10:00 a.m., playing records, switching on the newscasts, and reading local announcements; the next 4 hours were taken up with recording voiceovers and other off-air tasks. It could have become routine, but believing in the benefits she brought her listeners, Isisara started to go the extra mile. Each day, after her regular duties were over, she produced a 15-minute "mini show" of African history that included daily affirmations and meditations. Gradually she created a weekly variety show on topics she was interested in, adding artistic touches such as special sound effects to make the show "a little more captivating for the imagination," as she puts it. Her ratings were respectable, and the station's program director got involved in Baltimore politics and eventually became congressional representative and president of the National Association for the Advancement of Colored People. Life at the radio station was exciting. "We had a lot going on," Isisara recalls. "We felt we were the eyes and ears of the community in ways that commercial stations could not be."

This isn't to say that Isisara had anything against commercial media. For one thing, more people tune in to commercial radio and TV stations—and the pay is better. So after 5 years in public radio, Isisara started to think it was time to switch to the for-profit world. But as it turned out, making that switch wasn't as easy as she thought it would be.

Underestimating Obstacles

At first, Isisara figured she would get her foot in the door by volunteering at the local NBC television affiliate. "But they said no, they could only take college interns," Isisara recalls. So she did something very simple: She got around the system. She asked one of her former professors, who she kept in touch with, to sign her up for one of his college courses. That way she could qualify as a student intern and could apply for the intern position, which she easily got with her radio credentials.

With that hurdle passed, she had another: a hugely hectic schedule. Each morning Isisara would go to work at her radio station job and then rush to the TV station to do menial jobs, such as make copies and get coffee while the staff rushed around hurriedly putting together the evening newscast. It didn't feel worth it. Luckily, she impressed one of the TV anchors, Dorothy West, who did a morning show at the station. Who knows what it was that made West take Isisara under her wing and let her work as her intern, but Isisara's empathic, likable personality probably helped. Although the overnight hours were still hectic, with Isisara working all night to put together the morning show and then going to her own job with no break, now she felt like she was learning the ropes.

West taught her to listen to the police scanners for breaking news, how to write copy for television, and how to log film clips that went with the copy. "It was great for me," Isisara says. After working with West for 2 weeks, Isisara felt confident enough to apply for an entry-level position at the station as a production assistant. She interviewed for the job and got it.

In the high-stress atmosphere of a TV newsroom, people sometimes make mistakes. One memorable mistake happened when Isisara was news producer and had a new writer working for her. She'd given the writer several stories to complete, and the leads were done.

However, Isisara didn't realize the woman was still writing the stories even as the newscast began. Then the teleprompter got to a story that hadn't been written yet, and the anchors had to ad-lib as best they could. "We all learned something that afternoon," Isisara says. She took it as a learning experience for the writer, to learn to communicate when she was in over her head and for Isisara to keep more in touch with staffers. The writer went on to be a very good worker, and Isisara earned respect for being cool-headed and not placing blame. Once again, Isisara's empathy was an asset.

Once Isisara reached the level of news producer, an unlikely obstacle came her way: her husband died. It was a tough period. "By the time my husband died, I had buried every member of my immediate family," Isisara recalls. "I had two choices: I could keep living, or I could die myself. After a lot of soul searching, I decided while I'm still living it's my job to keep moving forward." And so she did.

Building Momentum—Empathetically

At this point in her career, when she was in her late 20s, Isisara's empathy and superb work ethic had earned her a great network. Hearing about her husband's death, one of her college mentors referred her for a new executive training program at Columbia Pictures. When she was invited to the program, she jumped at the chance to make a fresh start in a new city.

When Isisara was chosen for the program, she moved to New York City and began a series of 6-month rotations in different parts of Columbia's business. At the end of each rotation, she had to make a presentation to various executives at the company. "It was very nerve-wracking," Isisara remembers. On top of that, Columbia Pictures was sold to Sony while she was going through the leadership program. Her future at the new company felt unsure.

It was during her last rotation, in corporate affairs in Los Angeles, where she found her niche at the company. Corporate affairs, to Isisara, was how the company "presented its face to the world." With her background in radio and television news—and her natural way of being able to see other points of view—Isisara caught on quickly. One of the challenges for Sony at the time was to expand Columbia's facility in Culver City, a small community nearly surrounded by Los Angeles. Those expansion plans weren't always popular with local residents, Isisara saw, and part of the problem was that residents feared losing their historic architecture.

"Part of my job is to find ways to make nice with the local community," Isisara says. So she put herself in the shoes of residents, asked herself what would be a good-faith way to earn the trust and respect of the community. That's how she came up with her idea to sponsor a program where the corporation's executives and employees would volunteer to spruce up the city's schools. She convinced executives to suit up in overalls and go plant trees and paint school buildings. After all, just having lower-level employees do the work wasn't authentic, she saw. "It had to come from the heart of the company," Isisara says. It was a challenge to organize, but she pulled it together.

Isisara also saw that the entertainment industry was the face of America for much of the world, and often what the movies present are stereotypes that don't portray Americans in their best light. So she set out to expose Sony's workforce to broader ideas through something she dubbed the "Celebration of Culture." She brought in authors and performers from all parts of American culture. During the racial unrest in Los Angeles after the Rodney King verdict, Isisara brought in African entertainers. Her line of thinking was that if people could connect through music and art, they would see other people's humanity. Besides, it was fun.

Then the big earthquake of 1994 hit, and Isisara felt like it was time to move on. She started not to feel secure in L.A. and began looking for a way to move back to the East Coast.

Taking the Next Leap

Isisara found a job in Sony Music's New York offices, working in government affairs. Her boss knew about her corporate affairs work at Sony Pictures on the West Coast, and he was impressed. He told her he was grooming her to be his replacement when he eventually retired, but before he could retire he died abruptly without a clear succession plan. Isisara stepped forward and said she could fill his shoes, but senior management wasn't sure that she was ready.

That's when Isisara got her 10-month trial period as head of government affairs. Her triumph was something called the Tri-Caucus Retreat, a gathering attended by members of the U.S. Congressional Black, Hispanic, and Asian Caucuses.

The way she came up with the idea for the Tri-Caucus Retreat is such a great example of the benefits of walking in another person's shoes. While she was looking for a project to wow the people at Sony, Isisara attended a retreat for the Black Congressional Caucus Foundation board, of which she was a member. She met with the chairman and asked him what was the most important thing she could help him achieve. Notice she didn't ask him how he could help her. Instead she asked what he needed. His answer: better communication with other minority caucuses in Congress.

"I knew this was something I could do," Isisara remembers. With her background using entertainment to build bridges, she set up the Tri-Caucus Retreat as a way of having the three congressional caucuses meet on neutral territory and form personal connections. "It was the first time these members of Congress would be talking," Isisara says. "They work together in committees, but they're not necessarily communicating."

At the retreat, between the multicultural poetry readings and stage performances, there was time for sharing personal stories of why they got into public service. As the personal stories came out, connections were made. A California congresswoman who was the daughter of migrant workers could relate to an African-American congressman who was the son of a sharecropper. "It was so moving," Isisara says. "It was in that moment that I knew that these retreats were a success."

Isisara isn't sure what her next step is, but she knows it will be about building bridges. "The theme of my work is using art and culture to get people to see themselves and each other differently," Isisara says. "Then people treat each other differently, empathize with other people's point of view, and find common ground."

Walking in someone else's shoes is a powerful secret; try it and see where it takes you.

How to Walk a Mile in Their Shoes

Learning about the diversity of people around the globe gives you polish and widens your view of the world. Here are Isisara Bey's tips for how to open your mind.

- **Go to the movies...and art exhibits and lecture halls.** Use art and culture to expand your point of view: Read books by respected experts about subjects you know nothing about, attend concerts by performers from other cultures, or rent a foreign movie with subtitles.

- **Be curious.** Be genuinely interested in the people around you, especially in their thoughts and points of view. People love to talk about their interests, so you may make a new friend—and at the very least you'll probably learn something new.

- **Make allies.** We're all human, even when we have conflicting points of view. Try to find common ground and connect with people.

- **Know when to stand firm.** Just because you can see other people's points of view doesn't mean you always agree with them—especially when they don't believe in your abilities. Just take it as a chance to prove them wrong.

Wes's Worry Less Tip

► Is it *really* that bad?

Our worries have a way of shrinking when we see them in the bigger picture. When we open ourselves up to seeing the world around us, our problems seem smaller when compared to what's happening around the rest of the world. Think about it; people around the globe get through all kinds of problems— some of them life-threatening—every day. There are monstrous and devastating circumstances like famine, war, and illness, and people can face these with equanimity and courage. When you look at it that way, the annoying facts of the guy who's bucking for the promotion you want aren't nearly as daunting. Most of our worries are problems that we can solve; they're not insurmountable. And if we lose out on something we want, we can always try again. Ask yourself, "Is it really that bad?"

"Life is ten percent what happens to you and ninety percent how you respond to it."

—Lou Holtz

13

One Step Ahead

—Greg Downey (USOC, NBC Universal, and Coca-Cola)

It's not where you are right now that matters; it's where you want to be next. For Greg Downey, staying a step ahead of the game gave him a sizzling career in marketing and entertainment. He started out with a combination business and law degree and is now group director of entertainment at The Coca-Cola Company. If he hadn't thought ahead about where he wanted to be, his future might have been very different. "I could have ended up in some law firm writing people's wills," Greg says.

Not to say anything bad about lawyers who write wills, but Greg wanted a more exciting career than that. He always pictured himself working in marketing and doing something fun. Yet he valued the discipline of law school, so he consciously looked for a way to combine legal training with marketing and entertainment. His technique worked; in fact, he exceeded his dreams when he landed the job at Coca-Cola, the ultimate marketing company.

Careers are a lot like a game of pool. Most casual players are just thinking about the shot in front of them, just striking the cue ball and getting the next ball into the pocket. "But the really good players are thinking about the next shot," Greg says. "When you're making a shot, putting the ball in the pocket is only part of it. The other part is where the cue ball is going to end up when you put that ball in the pocket."

As Wayne Gretzky put it:

A good hockey player plays where the puck is. A great hockey player plays where the puck is going to be.

So it's important to maneuver your career so that the skills you're perfecting now will either allow you to move up in your current organization or will get you an even better offer elsewhere.

"If you're at a complete dead-end job, you should look at how to change that," Greg says. It's not enough to say, "Someday I'll have my boss's job." Really look at what people do in your division, how they add value to the company, and ask yourself where you want to be next. For Greg, those questions started in college.

Starting from Scratch

Like many young people, Greg wasn't sure what to major in during his undergraduate days. First, he considered pre-med, but he saw that he liked the business side of medicine better. He ended up with a degree in hospital administration. After some soul-searching, he noticed that a lot of politicians and leaders had law degrees—though they weren't necessarily practicing law at a firm. It's not necessarily their knowledge of the law that makes attorneys successful, but it's that they've all been through mental boot camp. They've learned problem solving and strategic thinking that trains them to stay two steps ahead of everyone else. This is something we can all do if we consciously keep our goals in mind.

It was a law school internship that jumpstarted Greg's career. Internships are very valuable, and they're not just for students. Even if you're no longer in school, an internship may still be a viable way to get you where you want to go. In Chapter 12, "Walk a Mile in Their Shoes," Isisara Bey enrolled in a college class years after she'd graduated and was out in the workforce, just so she could quality for an internship at a local television station. Alternatively, you can volunteer for a job. Many employers are disarmed when a job applicant tells them he or she will do anything just to get a foot in the door (see Kevin Noland, Chapter 6, "Be Distinct or Be Extinct"). For Greg, the internship that got his foot in the door was at Jim Kelly Enterprises, a business formed by Buffalo Bills quarterback Jim Kelly to handle his sports endorsements and charities.

Oddly enough, that internship connection came through when Greg had surgery for a shoulder injury. Coincidentally, Kelly had a similar sports injury, and they had the same doctor. Now it might sound unlikely that you get a chance to meet a professional athlete and arrange an internship, but life is full of coincidences. If we're focused on staying two steps ahead, we're much more likely to take advantage of these coincidences than someone who isn't focused. Greg had always wanted to be in sports and entertainment, so when he saw the chance, he grabbed it.

After Greg passed the New York bar exam on the first try (quite an achievement), the internship grew into a job as a vice president at Jim Kelly Enterprises. It was an amazing way to start his career, giving Greg contacts with media executives and marketers. After working there for 5 years, Greg also helped negotiate Kelly's retirement transition into a job as an NBC sports commentator. At that point, it seemed like a good time to move on. Greg had been a step ahead and thinking about his future after Kelly's retirement. During meetings with NBC, Greg met some guys who hooked him up with the marketing officer of the United States Olympic Committee (USOC). They were looking for someone to run sports marketing. This was in 1996 at the end of the Atlanta games. It was also the year Greg married.

"The day we got back from our honeymoon," Greg say, "we packed up and moved to Colorado Springs," headquarters of the Olympic Committee.

Underestimating Obstacles

In many countries, the governments pay for the training of the country's Olympic athletes—but not in the United States. The government doesn't give the Olympic athletes a penny. Instead, a congressional act gives the Olympic Committee legal oversight to license the Olympic trademark. In some circles, that kind of licensing is frowned upon as too commercial. But the way it's set up in the U.S., those licensing deals are the lifeblood of the Olympic training program.

As director of business development at the Olympic Committee, Greg worked to negotiate some new, creative marketing contracts. It was in 1996, right after the Atlanta games. Although today many of his accomplishments now seem to be everyday practices, at the time they were cutting edge—he was one step ahead in his work as well as in his career.

Corporate sponsors find the Olympic rings to be very valuable. Those linked rings represent fair play, success, and athleticism. It's a very powerful brand. But at the committee, sometimes it took a little persuading to change the minds of people who were used to doing promotions a certain way. For instance, in the lead-up to the Salt Lake City games, Greg suggested a whole new entertainment division to look at licensing rights for movies, instead of the old way of just getting television rights. Greg wrote up a business plan for it and convinced the right people. It wasn't a sea change, but it was a new idea. Greg led the effort, which was kicked off with *Miracle*, the movie based on the 1980 U.S. Olympic ice hockey team's victory over the Soviet Union at the Lake Placid winter games. It was a win.

Another innovation he came up with was to televise the inductions to the U.S. Olympic Hall of Fame. All the other Hall of Fame inductions—such as those for professional football and baseball—televise their ceremonies. People watch them, and sponsors pay for the chance to advertise. It seemed like common sense: Here are great athletes who everyone loves; however, no one had thought of doing this before. Greg recognized an unutilized asset, the induction ceremonies, and turned it into an entertainment property. Again, Greg was a step ahead.

Gradually, Greg was getting more and more interested in pure entertainment, instead of seeing things through the Olympic Committee lens. He dreamed of going to Hollywood. After the Salt Lake City games, he used his contacts with NBC—which had sponsored the Olympics—to get introduced to some network executives. It was a great move.

Building Momentum—Creatively

His next job was as vice president of business affairs at NBC, negotiating contracts with writers, directors, and actors, as well as handling marketing issues such as branding and product placements. He worked on the *Tonight Show* and *My Name Is Earl*. His first week in Los Angeles, Greg was in a temporary home while his wife and kids stayed in Colorado Springs working on selling their house and packing. "I was sitting on my back porch looking into the Hollywood Hills and thinking, 'Holy shit, I'm a Hollywood executive now. How did this happen?'"

The way he did it was by staying a step ahead and always looking to the next career move. His network of contacts had become so extensive that as his talents grew, and he was able to get himself noticed where he wanted to go. And it was a very satisfying career move. "I loved it," Greg recalls.

This was in 2003, when NBC was experimenting with product placement and brand integration. Basically, it's the new, creative approach to advertising that may replace the old 30-second commercial spots we all like to skip over with TiVo. Now most reality shows have their advertisers pay to integrate their products into the show—for example, having bottles of Heineken stocked in the fridge for the last episode of *The Real World*. The old way of thinking is to just blur out any and every product label—but now the opposite has taken place. As traditional advertisements continue to wane, networks look for opportunities to integrate products into their shows—from Marquis Jet in the first season of *The Apprentice* (see Chapter 18, "Exercise Your Middle Brain") to the Coca-Cola banner hanging in the background as *American Idol* contestants sing their hearts out to millions of viewers.

The entire landscape of product placement was in the "Wild West" era at the time. "There were no rules," Greg says. "It was like the Internet world in 1998. It was just wide-open sky. Everyone was just making it up as they went along." Only a few years later, product placement has really caught on and become part of the entertainment world. But Greg was a step ahead when the old guard still thought 30-second commercials should be the norm.

Taking the Next Leap

Greg worked hard to position himself as a creative thinker, but sometimes his own good education got in the way. Once, he was sitting in a brainstorming session where the senior executive running the meeting wanted them to come up with a name for a new production division. "We wanted it to be clever," Greg recalls. At the front of the room was a whiteboard filled with ideas that everyone in the room suggested. "Every idea I came up with, the senior executive treated as if it came from the kid's table," Greg recalls. The executive actually said something like, "Maybe we can just have Greg stick to the legal responsibility of looking up the names and checking them for copyright infringements." That got a rumble of laughter from the room. "I'm sitting there thinking, 'If no one in this room knew I was a lawyer, my ideas would be treated exactly like everybody else's,'" Greg recalls. He made note of that and pondered how to fix it.

Overall, his years at NBC were great. "I loved it," Greg says. But things were changing quickly in his life—he and his wife had children to think of. While he was at NBC, Coca-Cola called: "We have this entertainment division, and we'd like you to come run it. You're the perfect fit," they told him. It's hard to say no to an offer like that, but it was also hard to leave NBC. In the end, family concerns decided it. Even though they loved L.A., Greg and his wife agreed Atlanta, Coke's headquarters, would be a better place to raise kids.

Plus, Greg is having fun working with the Coke brand, which is an American icon and a marketing powerhouse. People there feel a certain enthusiasm for the beloved brand, he says, with its bright red logo and artful ads by illustrators such as Norman Rockwell.

And Greg doesn't always tell people he's a lawyer. "Then when people find out I'm a lawyer, it ends up they're surprised. It doesn't change their opinion of me." That may be because he's an upper-level executive now; but either way, he's staying one step ahead. By knowing what we want and thinking one step ahead, we can go for our wildest dreams.

Wes's Worry Less Tip

► **Attack the Mosquitos, then conquer the elephant.**

This is not only something that will help you worry less, this is a time-efficiency tip. The philosophy comes from a fellow named Dave Ramsey, a nationally syndicated radio host who helps listeners get out of debt. He advises listing your debts from the lowest to highest balance and to start attacking the smallest first—so that you see progress in eliminating debt. The same thing goes in prioritizing your day. I list the 15 things I have to do in my day, and it gives me a sense of peace and calm if I can knock out five or six of the small annoying things, the mosquitoes, quickly. We like to see that we're making progress; by attacking small manageable tasks early, you show yourself that you're already having a productive day. After you warm up on a few easy tasks, your mind is less cluttered with annoying "little stuff"—and you can concentrate on chores that matter the most and put food on the table.

"Get rid of the annoying mosquitoes first, then dissect the elephant."

—Wes Moss

Part IV
Take the Next Step

The next principle of the HUNT is "Take the next step." It's essentially the same whether you work for someone else or have your own business. The main difference when you work for someone else is that your steps are usually incremental and smaller than when you start your own business. Each step is less risk and less reward. With small business owners, one big step can mean the difference between poverty and landing on the cover of *Forbes*. When you ascend *within* an organization, the odds are on your side; you aren't risking your life savings when you undertake a new direction—but you're not gambling on launching the next Microsoft, either.

Even if you incorporate the entrepreneurial mindset at a large corporation, you always run the risk that you will stagnate—so taking little steps everyday is crucial! What you're after is maneuvering and carefully stepping from job to job, department to department, and title to title. Chronologically it's a slower climb for the duration of your career—30 or 40 years. Managing your career is a lifelong project.

The HUNT begins with harnessing what you have, underestimating your obstacles, and noticing your network. The last step is the key to the cycle: taking the next step—and always being *prepared* to take the next step! If you're not acting on the mental work from the initial three steps of the HUNT and making them manifest through *real* action steps—then you are standing still! Ask yourself, "What was the last *material* career or life step that I've taken lately?"

Dream

One of the secrets to taking steps is to break them down into doable pieces. For example, say you want to propose that you be put in charge of a new project at work. Visualizing how to do this is a great first step. Bob McDonald in Chapter 14, "Reminisce About Your Future," calls it "reminiscing about your future," and it's extremely powerful. Just be careful your visualizations don't get bogged down in negatives, imagining all the ways you could fail. It's fine to anticipate your boss's objections and come up with good answers. But sometimes the best answer is simple: Express how much you believe in the project and your ability to succeed.

Another way to jumpstart the process is to use your unconscious. Before I go to bed each night, I think about all the different parts of my life: my financial planning career, fatherhood, marriage, my financial radio show, and my relationships with friends and family. I put these ideas in my head so that my mind is open to having dreams about these parts of my life—dreams that may bring light to any current questions or problems that I might be facing—problems that my conscious thoughts have not yet figured out. Try it—it works!

Pen to Paper

Action steps require planning. The kind of planning I'm talking about here is action-oriented—number crunching and proposal writing, that kind of thing. For any project it's important that you do your homework and get a handle on the financial risks versus the rewards. It doesn't have to be too sophisticated, and you may have to pick a few numbers out of the air if you're going after something no one has ever done before. Even if it's full of estimates, there's something about having a proposal written down that makes it look more real when you share it with others.

In a group, having a plan on paper is also essential because there is usually a team of people to convince. If you were founder of a small startup, putting proposals in writing might not be as important because you're only convincing yourself. In a full-fledged company, a proposal also has another purpose: After the convincing is done, a written proposal can double as an action plan. When the plan is on paper, everyone can be on the same page.

Action

Here's the fun part: Do it! Bob McDonald (Chapter 14, "Reminisce About Your Future") got recruiters to chase him in a simple series of steps that consisted of writing articles and volunteering to speak at industry conferences about the kind of insurance coverage he marketed. Mylle Mangum (Chapter 16, "Ask Without Asking") sped up her rate of promotion by asking for the duties of the job above her, foregoing raises to the next pay grade until she proved she could do the job. GK Murthy (Chapter 15, "Nudge the Top Line") became a valuable partner at his company because he thought like an owner and regularly put together proposals for taking his company's software to other industries. When Vicki Gordon (Chapter 17, "Find the Need") hit a dead end in her hotel executive career, she created a proposal for a new position that would solve a company problem and proposed that she take that new position. Randy Brandoff (Chapter 18, "Exercise Your Middle Brain") researched a new way of conducting a newspaper insert ad campaign, carefully marketing to households of a certain income level—a job that helped his employer and his career.

Taking action requires you to take initiative and approach people. Knock on doors, make cold calls, ask your boss for a new opportunity, ask for that raise, do your career push-ups every day. What steps have you taken lately? How are you an object in motion? Have you written an article for an industry journal? Volunteered a proposal to your boss? Solved a customer or company need? We all have contributions to make. Make yours today.

Talk to People

The great thing about taking steps is that one step leads to another. As you go about taking one step, you get the idea for another step. And many times those ideas come because action gets you noticed; it helps you strike up conversations with coworkers or industry colleagues. And those conversations lead to more ideas for more steps forward. Once you get started, the ball just keeps rolling.

Put yourself out there and keep those conversations going. Stagnation is impossible if you are talking to people at lunch meetings, informal get-togethers, and civic groups. There's a whole world that opens up to us when we take action and get noticed.

Measure Your Progress

Keep track of your steps and every now and then measure them. It's great if your company already does quarterly reviews. If not, maybe you could ask your boss to institute them. Still, do your own informal measuring by reflecting back frequently on how far you've come. I heard of a man who every night reflected on his day—what he'd accomplished; what he wished he'd done; what he wished he could take back; and finally what he would do differently tomorrow. What a great idea.

The more action you take on, the smaller your mistakes seem—and the more easily you'll sleep at night. For instance, if you only take one or two new steps in your career this year, you'll be devastated if they don't work out. If you take 100 steps and see that 60 of them ended positively, the misfires and mistakes won't seem so huge. Measuring your progress is a great way to motivate yourself and keep the cycle of the HUNT constantly going and evolving. Get moving—you'll be glad you did.

When all is said and done, more is said than done.

—Lou Holtz

Hallmarks of People Who Take the Next Step

- They think big and dream and visualize their goals.
- They put pen to paper to sketch out a proposal and plan for what they're about to do.
- They take action. (Each day, you should do at least one thing to move yourself forward.)
- They talk to people. (Action will get you noticed, which will lead to conversations, which will lead to more ideas for action.)
- They measure their progress. (You need to honestly assess whether you are really going forward by regularly taking stock and looking at what you've done.)

Wes's Worry Less Tip

▶ Your body knows best.

I get antsy if I go any extended period of time without a good long run. Sure it's hard to find the time when you're in the middle of writing a book, growing your career, taking care of family life and a baby. It's not easy to get home before dark and exercise. For several weeks during the writing of this book, I just couldn't find time to do my much-needed workout. With every passing day I got more nervous and worried. As soon as I went for a run, I felt like the world's problems were solved. Don't let anything get in the way of staying fit and clearing your mind!

For motivation, try reading about fitness: I like *Men's Health* and *Best Life; Shape* and *Fitness* are my wife's favorites. You can't argue with your body's power to create natural endorphins, to be alert and calm at the same time. Whether you like running, swimming, tennis, cycling, yoga, or walking, exercise is just as important as psychotherapy and anti-anxiety medications. The funny thing is when I run, I automatically think of the most pressing questions and problems in my life and think through dozens of possible solutions. I come back from a run not only feeling better physically but also confident about how I can solve what's bugging me the most. Something powerful happens to your psyche when you sweat!

"It is exercise alone that supports the spirits and keeps the mind in vigor."

—Marcus Tullius Cicero

For more Worry Less Tips, visit www.wesmoss.com.

14

Reminisce about Your Future

—Bob MacDonald (Allianz Life)

One of the most interesting and revolutionary people I've ever talked to, Bob MacDonald, says the key to his success—or anyone else's—is the ability to reminisce about your future. It's a mantra he lives by and writes about in his fascinating books *Cheat to Win* (Paradon Publishing 2005) and *Beat the System* (Wiley 2007).

Most people, he explains, reminisce about memorable events in lives: their first kiss, the day they got married, or the birth of their first child. "And you reminisce in pictures. It's so vivid you can explain it to others and get them to understand it," Bob says. "Imagine how powerful you could be if you could reminisce about the *future* the way most people reminisce about the *past.*"

Bob isn't talking about predicting the future in some kind of visionary way; he's talking about *making* the future. Most successful entrepreneurs, he says, have the ability to see in their minds what they want to accomplish, what they want to happen. For Bob, he saw himself heading the division of a large, successful company by the time he was 30—and being president by the time he was 40. And even though he saw himself working his way up in a large organization—not starting his own company—he always saw himself as an entrepreneur.

"You don't have to go and start Microsoft to be an entrepreneur," Bob says. "You can be an entrepreneur managing a gas station or managing a department in a large company."

Bob said all this to me in the first 5 minutes of our talk, and he embodies much of what I'm trying to get across in this book—that it's possible to have the best of both worlds. While still being part of corporate America, Bob was at the same time in charge of his own destiny—without the startup risks of having his own business.

"The reason people want to be entrepreneurs is they want to control their lives," Bob says. "They want to have ownership of what happens to them. Many times where people aren't entrepreneurs they let others have control over their future, over their careers. If you allow that, you become bureaucratized, and other people control you."

After working for 10 years as an insurance agent in California, Bob saw that the path to the future he was reminiscing about—running his own division—would lead him to join the corporate world. So he took his first corporate job at age 32 as second vice president of marketing support at State Mutual. Even though he had a corporate title, Bob was determined to be unique. It was something he would swear by—and other people would swear at.

Starting from Scratch

In the staid, rigid culture of the financial services world, Bob knew he didn't fit in. First, he didn't have a college degree. Second, moving from Southern California to State Mutual's headquarters in Worcester, Massachusetts, Bob was an outsider from the West Coast in a world of Easterners where "out west" meant a trip to Buffalo. Instead of trying to fit in, he had another approach. "I had to go against the grain," Bob said. "I had to use entrepreneurial tactics within a large organization because that was the only thing that differentiated me from other people, the only thing that gave me a chance to be successful."

The problem at State Mutual, Bob found, was that most of the bright young staff were segregated from managers and executives. Anyone who entered the corporate offices encountered its rigid system, where executives sat in lavish offices at the center of the building, known as "the core," while everyone else sat in the surrounding cubicles. For most of the younger employees, the goal quickly became "to get into the core." Bob was different. He started in the core—in a lavish office with its own bathroom—but quickly wanted to get out.

Here's how he saw it: State Mutual's stuffy, structured system—where he felt so much an outsider—wasn't just getting in the way of his career aspirations. The rigid system was also getting in the way of teamwork and productivity at the company. And as second vice president of marketing support, Bob wanted to make his team shine.

"I'm trying to build this marketing organization within the company, and I had this philosophy that the people who are working for me are the ones who are going to make me successful," Bob says. But resentment toward the core created tension that undermined teamwork between him and his staff. So Bob decided to challenge the whole "core" office system.

This is what I love about Bob's story: He shows simple ways to be entrepreneurial even in a large organization. Instead of going with what's always been done, you can look at your job and ask yourself, "What are the problems here and how can I solve them?" Bob saw one of the biggest problems in his staff was morale. People couldn't stay focused on day-to-day goals because they were obsessed with a demeaning culture that told them they weren't worthwhile unless they were a manager. So instead of keeping track of marketing goals, his staff just wanted to find a way to "get into the core."

Bob's first entrepreneurial action started out small: He moved into a cubicle alongside the rest of his staff of 20. "I'm not worried about offices," he told the other executives. "I'm trying to get this job done. I felt the best way to do this was to get people unified."

On the day Bob moved into his cubicle, someone jokingly moved a porta-john into the cubicle—as if to substitute for the office with a bathroom that he had just moved out of. Bob took it all in stride, laughed, and took a photo of the porta-john. He still has that photo today.

Bob could laugh because that simple gesture of moving out of the executive offices gave him the building blocks of his corporate career. First, he learned an important lesson about how to win the loyalty of his staff; after he joined them in the cubicles, his staff was proud to work for him and was willing to work hard. Second, he brought reality into line with his "reminiscing" about being head of his own division. Instead of being an outsider, Bob became a cult hero among the State Mutual staff. Everyone knew about Bob, even the dismayed executives who liked being separate from the staff. With notoriety and a strong team, Bob was on his way to being a leader.

Underestimating Obstacles

"If you can't be one of them, beat 'em," Bob tells me. He is in his 60s now, but the exuberance in his voice gives me a glimpse of how much he enjoyed bucking the system during his career. You may not have to be as much against the system as Bob, but his energy and the way he approaches obstacles are essential to an entrepreneurial mindset.

Not everyone in this book tells stories of bucking the system— with gusto—as much as Bob. In fact, some people—such as Mylle Magnum in Chapter 16, "Ask Without Asking"—are clearly team players who honor company traditions. But while Bob and Mylle seem like they take opposite approaches—one against corporate tradition, and the other embracing it—they have this in common: tackling obstacles with energy and optimism. Obstacles are for jumping over.

Here was Bob, sitting in his cubicle and working with his team to market a new insurance product called TLC, Total Life Coverage. And he was planning how to get his career moving. Bob had a team that was willing to work hard, thanks to his gesture of sitting among them. "They worked their asses off!" is how Bob puts it. He loved going to work, and he had fought against a system that other employees felt controlled by. But it was also becoming clear to him that State Mutual had a long line of people in front of him who wanted to be president. And even if he could do a great job marketing Total Life Coverage, he wasn't going to get to the top anytime soon.

Instead of cursing his fate—an outsider with no college degree—Bob leapt right over that obstacle. "I'd achieved a lot but wasn't going to be president," he says. "I knew I was going to have to go somewhere else."

So Bob set about a campaign to get more visibility within the insurance industry. He did this by going to conferences and conventions and speaking about the Total Life Coverage concept and by writing articles about it. Again, Bob didn't make the traditional step of contacting a headhunter and trying to chase after a new position. "It's like that old saying: 'When you're getting run out of town, get in the front and make it look like a parade,'" Bob says. "I wanted to make it look like *they* were chasing *me.*"

Building Momentum—Heroically

Of course, Bob did get chased.

After only two and a half years at State Mutual, Bob was hired as chief marketing officer at ITT Life in Minneapolis. Although the company wasn't as stodgy as State Mutual, ITT was like most financial services and insurance companies at the time: pretty bureaucratic. "The only way that we could make ITT Life successful was by making it an entrepreneurial culture within a very bureaucratic system," Bob says.

His first innovation: Once each quarter, all 640 employees would go to a theatre in the building's basement where they would be presented with the company's financial report. Not everyone liked that. "They said, 'Don't do this. People shouldn't have this kind of information. They should just be happy to have a job,'" Bob recalls. "I just ignored them. The thing with the bureaucrats is if you're successful, they have no power over you. Only when you fail do they have power."

And Bob didn't plan on failing.

"One of my philosophies is, you don't move up in a corporation by kissing the asses of the people above you, but by supporting the people you work with and allowing them to push you up," Bob says. So, still the cult hero, Bob kept up the financial meetings and other innovations aimed at uniting everyone in the company toward a common goal: getting a bigger chunk of the life insurance business.

At the time, 1977, ITT Life was "the dregs of the insurance business," as Bob describes it. They were outside the mainstream of the industry and made most of their money from long-term care, Medicare supplement policies, and cancer policies—things that Bob calls "scraps from the dinner table."

Bob's leadership style worked, and he achieved results. And the small, struggling company was a great place to rise to the top. As he provided results, he quickly moved up to chief marketing officer and then chief operating officer. Two and a half years after taking the job at ITT Life, Bob was president. (Two years ahead of his plan to be president by age 40.) It was the kind of fast movement that he couldn't have made at top-heavy State Mutual. Even though ITT Life was struggling, Bob saw it as an opportunity—in true entrepreneur style.

"My job was to turn the company around. Have it grow and become much more successful," Bob says. So he rolled up his sleeves and started living the job he'd been reminiscing about all his life.

Taking the Next Leap

Even though Bob was president, ITT Life was just a small piece of a large conglomerate: ITT Holdings. The group owned several mostly unrelated businesses, such as Sheraton, Hartford Insurance, and Interstate Bakeries. ITT Life was under Hartford's management because it was in the same industry, but the relationship wasn't always in ITT's best interests, at least not as Bob saw it.

Even though he'd made his goal of president, Bob wanted to be president of something great, something successful. He wanted to change a company that wasn't even in the mainstream into a company that was a focal point of the life insurance industry.

His approach was classic: He made an enemy. And the enemy was the insurance industry itself.

Back in the early 1980s, it was an open secret in the financial industry that whole life insurance wasn't a very good product anymore. Many financial institutions and investment firms were selling more updated products. But within insurance companies whole life was still the Holy Grail. Bob likes to say that insurance companies were competing *with* each other, against investment firms and financial institutions. Bob was about to change that and have the insurance companies compete *against* each other.

So one morning in 1982, Bob stood up at a press conference and made an announcement that turned him into the "antichrist" of the insurance industry. "I announced that whole life insurance, the backbone of the insurance industry, was obsolete, out of date, and in fact a consumer rip-off," Bob recalls. "We're going to stop selling it because we think it's anti-consumer, and we're going to sell a different product."

Bob was bucking the system yet again.

He was even thrown out of an insurance industry association. Did he care? It doesn't sound like it. "Suddenly this company that no one knew about was getting front page stories in the *Wall Street Journal* and the *New York Times,* saying that whole life is no good," Bob says. "Well, people outside the industry had been saying that for years. But when the president of a life insurance company comes out and says this product isn't good, it makes news."

All the personal attacks didn't bother Bob because he wasn't being dishonest. In fact, he figures the counter attacks showed that he was right. "The irony is the other insurance companies attacked what we were saying, not because we were wrong but because we said it. That just created more publicity. If someone is raving and raving and everyone ignores them, it goes away." So the more Bob and ITT Life were attacked, the better business became for ITT Life.

"Our insurance company started growing. It became highly recognizable. It was considered the leader of the revolution," Bob says.

Many people were probably surprised at this upstart, but Bob really wasn't. Early on in his career he had "reminisced" or envisioned himself at the helm of a successful company or division. A luxurious office didn't lull Bob into a false sense of complacency. He remained driven by the image of himself running a successful company. He's really not surprised that that's what happened.

After 7 years at the helm of ITT Life, Bob did eventually go on to start up his own insurance company (LifeUSA), grow it, and sell it. The last position he held was CEO of Allianz Life, a post he retired from in 2002. I think the way he jumped from mid-level management to upper-level shows the power of reminiscing about—and owning— your future. So go ahead and make some "memories" about the future you want for yourself. As Bob says: "*Make* history, or you'll *be* history."

Think Big, Really Big!

Take a page from Bob McDonald's playbook and learn how he "reminisces about the future." He sums it up in these steps:

- **Write it down.** The legendary Lou Holtz is the only coach in the history of college football to take six different teams to a bowl game, win five bowl games with different teams, and have four different college teams ranked in the final Top 20 poll—not to mention winning a national championship in 1998 while coaching the Notre Dame Fighting Irish.

  However, at the age of 28 he found himself unemployed, out of money, and completely dejected with life. After reading *The Magic of Thinking Big*, by David Schwartz, in 1966, he decided to write down all his wildest life goals. The goals included meeting the president and the pope, coaching Notre Dame football, winning a national championship, appearing on the Johnny Carson show, and hitting a hole-in-one. In total, Holtz wrote down 107 goals. Pretty ambitious for an unemployed 28-year-old.

  Last time I checked, Holtz had completed 81 of his life goals—the pope, the president, Notre Dame, a national championship, and a pair of holes-in-one!

- **Visualize it.** If you can see it, and believe it, it will come. Each night before you fall asleep, visualize your top three business or career goals. See them and go through them in your mind as if they have already happened.

- **Read about it.** In the best selling book *The Secret* by Rhonda Byrne, she and a vast array of leadership experts describe the power of belief and visualization and how they allow you to "attract" anything and everything you want. It's hard to argue with the results.

Need help rallying the troops to "think big?" Wes may be able to help…for more information, visit www.wesmoss.com.

Wes's Worry Less Tip

► Stop extrapolating your problems!

Little worries tend to mushroom into big ones if we let them. For instance, I noticed a small crack in the brick on my front step where a leaky pipe had softened the ground beneath our porch. A plumber came out and said that I may have a sinking foundation; eventually the crack could travel up the whole house, and we'd need to replace the roof. Turns out—it's nothing that a handful of cement won't fix.

Whether you're talking about a home repair or a glitch in the global economy, human beings tend to take today's small event and extrapolate it into a trend for tomorrow. Unemployment picks up, and we start to think unemployment will go up forever. If the stock market goes up, we think it will keep going up and make us all rich. My point is, 90 percent of the time our extrapolations are just plain false. When things happen—a hiccup in global equity markets, earning a commission check, a flat tire—just take it for what it is. A flat tire doesn't mean your car is falling apart. One event doesn't define the future.

"Men do not stumble over mountains, but over mole hills."

—Confucius

15

Nudge the Top Line

—GK Murthy (Sierra Atlantic)

GK Murthy could have been a successful project manager who slowly worked his way up the pay scale. Instead, GK nudged his employer off the fence, helped the company grow from 60 to 1,200 employees, and made both himself—and his boss—rich.

When I think about Silicon Valley, I think high tech, high achieving, and high stress. But when I talked to GK, the first thing I noticed was how relaxed he was. Sure, he gets excited when he talks about his successes, but he's a very calm, down-to-earth kind of guy. Maybe that's because he's found the *best of both worlds:* the middle ground between the 9-to-5 rat race and the risky world of the entrepreneur. And it's easy to see that the way he found that middle ground was to think like an owner and nudge up profits.

The first nudge came a few months into his job at Sierra Atlantic, a Silicon Valley consulting firm. GK had just moved to the U.S. from India and was used to working for large American companies with projects in Asia. But Sierra Atlantic was small. GK was a little worried about what it would be like at such a small company. "That was my initial feeling, but pretty soon the work was so challenging, it was something I wanted to do," GK says. And as he got immersed in the project, GK noticed something: The software they were writing could lead to a whole way of selling products to new industries. "I realized we were actually sitting on top of a goldmine," GK says.

Now, it's not rocket science to come up with ways to help your company make more money. Let's face it. Most of us, as we do our jobs day after day, end up coming home thinking, "Wow, this company could be so much more profitable if only..." And then we do nothing about it. And the reason we do nothing about it is because we don't want to fail. And of course, when we stick our necks out, failing is a very real possibility. As Bob MacDonald says in the previous chapter, if you take a risk and it works out, everything is fine—but if you take a risk and fail, you're fired.

What's so great about GK's story is that he's proof you can take risks without putting your head on the chopping block. It's all in the art of the nudge.

Starting from Scratch

The first step in becoming good at "nudging" is to see the big picture. GK learned to have an ownership mentality during the 10 years before he came to Sierra Atlantic, when he was designing hardware and software in Asia. His jobs had taken him to factory floors where he supervised people using the products he designed. So GK was a hands-on kind of guy. When he designed something, he didn't just do it well—he thought about the people who were going to use it. By the time he came to Sierra Atlantic, seeing the big picture was second nature.

So GK's talent for seeing the big picture made him a very good consultant and project manager at Sierra Atlantic, but it wasn't enough. Sure, he was great at managing projects, but GK's big-picture attitude could have also made him dissatisfied because someone who's used to seeing the big picture isn't going to be satisfied managing one project at a time at a small consulting firm. GK could have worked there for a while, gotten bored, and jumped to the next employer, like so many other talented people in Silicon Valley. That's why his second step is so important.

The second step is to pretend you own the place. That means looking at your job or project as if it were your own little company. GK, only a few months on the job, was thinking like he owned the place. So when he was working on a project—writing a few lines of code for an Oracle product—he thought, why don't we market this kind of work to other customers? "Buying software isn't the end of the solution. You have to implement it," GK explains. "Anytime you buy software, it only answers part of your business problems. Large companies, they buy the software, but they need to do a ton of work outside of the software to run their business." GK saw the goldmine: Sierra Atlantic could sell their services to do that "ton of work" outside the software.

GK didn't do what so many of us might have done—just do his job and go home. Or, worse, grumble about Sierra Atlantic being a small-time company compared to the big guns he'd worked for before. Instead, GK saw that plenty of companies would be glad to have Sierra Atlantic come in and tweak their Oracle or SAP software and make it really work well for them. And right away, he went to tell the boss.

GK sat down and told the company's founder, Raju Reddy, his ideas about selling Sierra Atlantic's services to customize off-the-shelf software for other companies. This might sound like a brash thing to do, but think about it: If you start a company, your main motivation is to make money. If someone comes along with ideas for how you can make *more* money, the boss is going to listen. Especially if you handle it like GK, who wasn't pushy and wasn't calling the company's old way of doing business stupid; he just wanted to nudge the company toward growing and making more money. Here's the thing: Bosses like to be nudged, especially when you have an idea about how to bring in more money.

"Raju was very receptive to this," GK remembers. "He likes to encourage people to think independently." GK doesn't think about that first step—taking an idea to the boss—as earth-shaking. But GK's first step was about to change things in a big way.

Underestimating Obstacles

Another important step in the art of the nudge: Believe in your-self, but don't bet the farm. That's because no matter what, nobody bats 1000. So GK didn't set himself up to fail by saying that huge numbers of companies would hire Sierra Atlantic to customize their software for them. Instead, GK quietly put together reasonable pro-posals for companies he was familiar with from his previous jobs in Asia. Sometimes the proposals worked, and sometimes they didn't. Either way, every company that he approached who signed on was new business Sierra Atlantic wouldn't have found otherwise.

Just because he didn't bet the farm doesn't mean GK didn't take risks. He took plenty. Like the time he met someone at a social gath-ering who knew how to provide software support for an older kind of mainframe computer. It just so happened that GK had been courting a boat manufacturer that had the same kind of mainframe computer. The only catch was that Sierra Atlantic didn't have anyone on staff who knew how to work with that particular mainframe. GK got the guy hired for Sierra Atlantic—at a $100,000 annual salary. Then, GK turned around and gave the boat manufacturer a proposal to provide maintenance and support for its mainframe. It worked. Sierra Atlantic won the contract.

And then there was the time when GK put together a proposal to maintain and support software for a mid-sized specialty chemicals company in New York. In the chemicals industry, where processes are streamlined and controlled by computer software, it's vital that everything runs smoothly, GK explains. Even little glitches cost money. So GK's proposal was about getting rid of one of the glitches.

There was only one problem: Sierra Atlantic didn't have a software maintenance program.

But GK, who always thought like he owned the company, believed in Sierra Atlantic's ability to do the job, and he underestimated the chance of failure. He believed in Sierra Atlantic so much that he was able to convince the guys from the chemical company. "They saw the passion and honesty that we brought to the table," GK says, "so they awarded us the contract."

Within 9 months, GK had nudged the top line so much that he was promoted to "director of process industry verticals." How many verticals did Sierra Atlantic have? None. GK's was the first. "They pretty much created this standalone unit for me," GK recalls.

Now GK had what he'd been pretending to have: his own little business within a business. And he knew just what to do with it.

Building Momentum—Passionately

One of the first things GK needed was a staff. That's because at first he was director of a brand-new division of Sierra Atlantic, but that division existed on paper only. Soon, it would have 100 employees: "I pretty much recruited every one of them myself," GK says. Finding people to work for him was a job in itself, but GK was enthusiastic. All he had to do, he says, was find people like himself who had a passion for the company.

"It's the passion that matters a lot," GK says. "If passion for the job isn't there, the chance of succeeding isn't good."

Sometimes, GK would hire people he met at social events. Sometimes he would convince people he already knew. No matter where

he was, GK was looking for passionate people with computer skills—
the kind of person a client would enjoy working with.

And quite a few of GK's hires were in India, where Sierra Atlantic
runs its outsourcing operations. When hiring in India, GK used a
clever technique that Sierra Atlantic had come up with: include the
parents. That's because in India parents are much more involved with
their children's lives; adults will even go to their parents to ask their
opinion about whether they should take a job. So Sierra Atlantic
would hold recruiting parties and invite the parents.

Little by little, GK built a staff in which he had confidence. Many
of those hires are still with the company today. He says: "If I look back
on my own career, one of the things I feel proud about is the number
of people I brought into this organization."

As he built a staff—and built confidence among clients—GK
found yet another way to nudge the top line.

Taking the Next Step

Earlier in this book I talked about the importance of the Triple
Rs: Repeatable, Reoccurring Revenue. It's a simple idea. What it
boils down to is that you earn money even when you're sleeping. In
the case of Linda Rabb (Chapter 1, "The Compound Income
Effect"), who sells Aflac insurance, the three Rs have to do with earning commissions and renewals on the policies she sells. In GK's case,
he earned significant portions of company stock; one day, when Sierra
Atlantic is either sold or goes public with a stock offering, GK will be
able to reap those rewards.

The three Rs are important to companies as well as individuals,
and GK found a way for Sierra Atlantic to get in on the three Rs
by selling its services in a new annuity contracts. The way it works is

instead of just writing some computer code and getting paid once, Sierra Atlantic would do a computer project and then maintain that software and hardware for an annual fee. For Sierra Atlantic, annuity contracts help alleviate the "feast and famine" cycle that is so common in consulting businesses. When GK started this in 2002, Sierra Atlantic had *one* annuity contract; now such contracts make up a huge chunk of its business.

GK also came up with another way to nudge up the top line: buying the competition. It happened in 2005 when GK was running some of Sierra Atlantic's new business lines in Europe. The company had won some business, but growth was slow, and competition was fierce. One competitor, Iterion, was especially tough to beat. "I was getting uncomfortable," GK says. Then he came up with an idea: buy Iterion. So far, GK says, that seems like it was a good move.

GK still works at Sierra Atlantic, and now his title is Senior Vice President of Enterprise Solutions. When he tells people at parties in Silicon Valley that he has worked for the same company for 10 years, "They can't believe it. They think I must be one of the founders," GK says. That's because in Silicon Valley companies—as in many companies today—people get dissatisfied and move around from employer to employer. GK has escaped this rat race by cultivating a position for himself at Sierra Atlantic where he gets a piece of the pie—and a reason to stay.

People have a lot of words for someone like GK: rainmaker, mover and shaker, trailblazer, wheeler and dealer. GK's story shows us how we can take our good ideas and turn them into gold for our employers—and ourselves. GK shows us that with a passion for your work and confidence in yourself, you can nudge the top line and find the best of both worlds: the comfort of a job with benefits and the wealth-making ability of a company founder. So try being a rainmaker, and the best of both worlds could be within reach for you too.

Nudge the Top Line

When you take the initiative to increase the company's business, even if it's not one of your job duties, you make yourself that much more valuable. GK Murthy shares his tips for how to do this:

- Pay attention to the big picture. Notice *how* your employer brings in money.

- Pretend you own the place. When you see new ways to make money, work at making them happen.

- Bring your boss on board.

- Surround yourself with people who are passionate about the work the company does.

- Make sure you are compensated for the new income streams you bring in.

Wes's Worry Less Tip

▶ There's no substitute for preparation.

Even the best of us worry if we have to wing it and we're not prepared. Taking risks is a must in business, but when you're unprepared you will lie awake in bed at night sweating over something as small as tomorrow's five-minute talk at the weekly sales meeting. However, if you have outlined your argument, rehearsed your major point, and know your topic—however long that may take—the nervous butterflies will be cut by 90 percent or more. For example, GK Murthy did his research before he approached a boat manufacturer regarding their mainframe computer system. He researched what kind of system the company had, found several possible solutions to their problems, and even hired an employee with the know-how to provide that support. After doing those extra steps, GK had positioned Sierra Atlantic to provide the new service as if they were the perfect fit for the job all along. He had the answers before the client asked the questions. No wonder he wasn't worried!

Linda Rabb (Chapter 1) believes in research and preparation so much that she loads her presentation material in her car two days before a sales meeting. The theme behind this book is pushing the envelope, asking for more of yourself and from your employer; that's going to create anxiety. The best way to conquer that is to be prepared before you make presentations or take on new projects. This way, you're not feeding your fears of failure. You can be confident and unworried, knowing you've done your homework.

Success depends upon previous preparation, and without such preparation there is sure to be failure.

—Confucius

16

Ask Without Asking

—Mylle Mangum (GE and IBT)

This chapter is for modest, hard-working people who just want to put down their heads and throw themselves into a job they love—people who want to get noticed for doing a great job. Most of the time, I have to admit, just working hard isn't enough. Unfortunately, as Linda Rabb's story in Chapter 1, "The Compound Income Effect," shows, employers are notorious for taking advantage of hard-working people and paying them just enough to keep them coming back to work every Monday morning. But being an outsider who shakes things up—like Bob MacDonald—isn't a strategy that will work everywhere. So Mylle's story offers a middle way: If you find the right employer—one who appreciates entrepreneurial thinking and hard work—you can build a great career and a decent amount of wealth.

Mylle, who started her career at General Electric more than 35 years ago, says her philosophy working in large corporations was to let her work speak for itself: "I always got a job and got paid *after* I'd done it," Mylle says. This is similar to the attitude I've heard from entrepreneurs who run their own companies: They create a reputation for great value first, and then the monetary success follows. In a corporate job—in a company that values employees' contributions—money rewards come each year at the annual review. Setting yourself up to be in a great position at these reviews requires the kind of overachieving that Mylle is great at. By finding solutions to business problems, Mylle would ask for more money without actually asking.

193

When she started out as a computer programmer for GE in 1972, Mylle didn't know she'd stumbled onto a job with an entrepreneurial company. Really, GE wasn't all that entrepreneurial at the time by some people's reckoning. Mylle had a degree in education and psychology, an internship working with juvenile delinquents, and a short stint teaching gifted children, but she was seeking new challenges. Mylle became aware that GE was hiring, and she got an entry-level job at GE as a computer programmer.

Obviously, Mylle was not a traditional hire, or as she likes to say, "I think I was hired for entertainment value." But, seriously, Mylle probably got the job because she told the interviewer she would teach herself how to program computers. "I told them, 'If I can't learn, I'll quit before you ever have to fire me.'" That's a gutsy thing to say.

From the beginning, Mylle started off with that refreshing attitude: She would learn whatever she had to in order to accomplish her job. Little did she know, at the time, GE executives were going through some learning of their own. Jack Welch, who would become CEO in 1981, was shaking up the ranks. He'd nearly quit GE in 1961 when, as a young engineer, he felt stifled by the company's bureaucracy and underappreciated by his boss. When an executive persuaded him to stay, promising a small-company environment, Welch stayed on. As he outlines in his book, *Jack: Straight from the Gut,* Welch understood how frustrating it was to work in a bureaucracy, so he created an entrepreneurial, small-company atmosphere at the GE behemoth.

All Mylle knew was that in her job as a programmer, she would work on different aspects of GE's locomotive business. With youthful enthusiasm, Mylle cheerfully dug in to learn how to be a computer programmer. And with each problem she tackled and solved, she was asking for more challenges and more responsibility. Her style was to give value that was one step ahead of her paycheck, and then the paycheck—fueled by performance bonuses and raises—would constantly catch up with her. It might not work everywhere, but at the right company it can be a clever strategy.

Starting from Scratch

As a modest person, Mylle says her success at GE "had a lot to do with youth and stupidity." After dealing with juvenile delinquents, she says, programming computers just "didn't seem hard." Here she was, far from where she'd grown up in sunny Georgia, working at GE's location in Erie, Pennsylvania, where she was steeped in manufacturing and computers. Instead of being intimidated, Mylle says, "It was fabulous to learn." And what she learned was that "computers are just tools for getting results."

From the beginning, Mylle loved how computers could be used to track and map the business to be more and more efficient. At the time, the 1970s, technical people tended to get "put in corners by themselves," Mylle says. But Mylle wasn't in love with programming; she was more enthusiastic about how to use the technology to build locomotives. "I worked hard to relate technology to results," Mylle says. "The way you put the locomotive together was you brought in parts and moved the pieces through the factory. I got very good at figuring out how to do it better."

Throughout her first 7 years at GE, Mylle was part of the team that was battling to increase the company's market share in the locomotive industry. GE's strategy was relentless innovation that competitors couldn't keep up with. Thanks to hard work from people like Mylle, GE crowded out the competition by bringing market share up from 12 percent to 70 percent throughout the 1970s. There's even a book written about how the locomotive industry changed dramatically throughout the twentieth century, with GE being the winner.[1]

So Mylle got herself noticed. From her point of view, she was a good team player, tackling problems and pushing herself to learn new

---

[1] Churella, Albert. *From Steam to Diesel: Managerial Customs and Organizational Capabilities in the Twentieth Century American Locomotive Industry.* Princeton University Press: Princeton, New Jersey. 1998.

things along the way. But I have to emphasize how important it was that she worked for a company that valued the entrepreneurial approach. She didn't have to buck the system, like Bob MacDonald in the insurance industry (Chapter 14, "Reminisce About Your Future"), because GE executives were already shaking up the old ways of doing things—using new technology and an enlightened company culture. In Mylle's case, it was more important to be a team player and join the program.

Unfortunately, someone like Mylle—who says she never directly asked for a bonus or a raise—could have been eaten alive in a less innovative company culture. That's why when I tell Mylle's story, I keep mentioning you should choose your employer wisely. Look up case studies and research what companies are getting results. For instance, a case study of the locomotive industry by Albert Churella mentions that GE's managerial style was what won out over General Motors' more traditional culture. Both companies had access to the same technology, but GE's culture helped it adopt technology faster and with better results. The key to Mylle's success is tied to the fact that she was working for a company with a culture that recognized results and valued hard work.

Underestimating Obstacles

All around her at GE, Mylle saw change: new technology, new bosses, new ways of doing things. After all, her whole job at GE (as computer programmer and then systems analyst) was finding new ways of doing things. And all around her, Mylle saw the old guard of GE employees dismayed with all the change. "When I started at GE, there was still a sense of fraternity. People worked for one company for all those years," she says. "I was on the front end of the transformation. You learn a tough lesson, that it isn't secure." Mylle was beginning her career at a moment in history when the idea of working for one company all your life was giving way to today's reality: careers with a patchwork of different employers. Mylle learned early that if she could find new ways of doing things—find ways of getting over obstacles—she would always have a job, somewhere.

"I'll never design a nuclear power plant," Mylle says, "but can I figure out the dynamics, the drives, the markets." That's the kind of confidence she learned while analyzing systems at GE.

Mylle was willing to take chances when she hit obstacles—both in her day-to-day job and in her career advancement.

In her day-to-day job, for instance, one of the risks she took was to push for GE products to always be better than the competitors'. For instance, if her analysis found that a GE system could cut costs by 30 percent by using non-GE circuit breakers, she would work with her teams to improve the GE product to achieve equal if not greater efficiency than the competitors'. She would continue to support the company policy of using GE products while also finding ways to reduce costs and increase efficiency.

In her career, her way of approaching barriers was to ask for a challenge *without* asking for a raise. This is maybe what makes being an entrepreneur inside a corporation so different from being an entrepreneur on your own: You have to be a team player. Mylle says her way of getting ahead would go something like this: She would ask for the duties of the job above her—without the increase in salary. She would say, "You don't have to pay me for it, just give me the opportunity to show what I can do." Again, in a different kind of company this could backfire, leaving you with no free time and little salary. But at a place like GE, where performance bonuses and raises were handed out by merit, it worked great.

Mylle's volunteering to take charge of projects worked for her because being the one in charge—the person who is accountable for getting a job done—is the one who reaps the most benefit. After 7 years of programming and analyzing systems, Mylle was rewarded with a promotion to GE's corporate consulting business. She went from building better locomotives to working on all of GE's major businesses: nuclear, power distribution, factory automation. It's a good thing she saw change as positive because changes were coming.

Building Momentum—Sanely

Working in corporate consulting for GE, Mylle's work was pitted against big-league consultants such as McKinsey—so it was high-level competition. And it was gratifying when her team's analysis won out. There where hits and misses along the way, which Mylle is hesitant to talk about, even now, because of her great loyalty to GE. But Mylle learned that no matter what happened in her job, her security didn't count on always kicking a field goal.

"Security comes from within," says Mylle, who thrived in the high-pressure world of consulting. "Even though I did well in this environment, you can't take that for granted. My work is not who I am. Be very careful that you don't get that intertwined, that company is your identity. Psychologically that gets dangerous. People attach too much to their business." That, in a nutshell, is a powerful statement about how to get through corporate America without getting bogged down. And I'll bet it did more for Mylle than just keep her sane. Mylle's upbeat attitude made her likeable.

In *The Tipping Point,* Malcolm Gladwell talks about what he calls *connectors*, people who help trends catch on. The way they do this is by having more acquaintances and friends than usual. For fun, he has a little test to figure out whether you are a connector: It's a simple list of names from the Manhattan phone book. As you read through the list of names, you note how many people you know who share the same last names. If you know more than 50 or so, you're a connector.

I didn't give that test to Mylle, but if I did I'd bet she'd be a connector. That's because she sprinkled our conversation with names of people she'd met along the way who might fit in my book. It dawned on me as we talked that this was probably another reason for her success. Not only is Mylle modest, she's also upbeat and nice to talk to—you can tell she genuinely likes to help people in any way she can.

Throughout her career at GE, which included tenures in systems, manufacturing, sales, and marketing, Mylle kept asking for challenges—and mostly meeting them. And she kept her sunny disposition.

Taking the Next Step

As a schoolteacher-turned-computer-programmer, Mylle didn't just learn technical things at GE. She learned how to take risks and how to lead. "It was as simple as knowing when to jump and when to step out," Mylle says. Managing small groups of the company, she learned that "leading is not always telling people what to do. Managing is sometimes by example. It is sometimes by goal-setting, sometimes by energy level, and sometimes by doing the tough things."

One of the tough things was knowing when to look outside the company for advancement. In 1985, Mylle got an offer from Bell-South to put together its international business strategy. And she took the job. It was the opportunity of a lifetime; BellSouth had just been divested from AT&T through a federal antitrust action. BellSouth, no longer a part of AT&T or privy to its business plans, had to build its international business plans from scratch. For someone from GE, which had a huge international business, it was amazing to Mylle that the international business plan had to be built from scratch. But like she always did, Mylle dug into the job, and within a year she was president of BellSouth International.

After she reached that level of expertise, Mylle's success was pretty much guaranteed. She went on to senior management positions at Holiday Inn and Carlson Wagonlit Travel. Now she's owner and CEO of IBT, a company specializing in designing, building, and consulting for financial services and specialty retailers. But even if she hadn't risen to that level, she's proof that you can be an entrepreneur inside a huge corporation—and keep your sanity—if you learn how to impress the right people.

So as you think about Mylle's story, try to make comparisons to the company where you work now. Is your employer more like Bob McDonald's first job, where executives were segregated from the rest of the workforce—even using separate bathrooms? Or is your employer more like Mylle's, where even a beginning computer programmer—driven to work hard and find solutions—could rise through the ranks? Most employers are probably somewhere in between, so Mylle's power to ask (and receive) *without* asking can be a lesson to us all.

Wes's Worry Less Tip

► You're just NOT that busy.

Being "too busy" is one of the most frequent complaints we all hear, and it has a way of compounding our worries. After all, if we're too busy to even attend to our career—our very livelihood—how can we get ahead? My answer to that is you're just NOT that busy. A busy life should be a life filled with rich, rewarding things—not an excuse for ducking responsibility. Look at what is really getting in your way, and you might find "being too busy" is just an excuse. The best business professionals operate in a storm of clutter; in fact that's a key business success. Don't think for one minute that an executive vice president traveling around the world with responsibility for thousands of employees isn't busier than you. Don't think the mother dealing with three kids, getting her degree at night, and working full time isn't busier than you. No matter how crazy you think your life is, there are lots of people who would look at your schedule with envy.

"If you want something done, ask a busy person to do it."

—Lucille Ball

17

Find the Need

—Vicki Gordon (IHG)

Everyone needs something. Companies need people with skills to conduct business each day. People need jobs. So the way to get ahead in an organization is to find out what the company needs and then ask yourself how you can fulfill that need. That's the strategy Vicki Gordon put together in her 35-year career in the hotel industry. It's gotten her up to the level of senior vice president of corporate affairs at Intercontinental Hotel Group, a hotel conglomerate that includes 3,800 hotels worldwide. Pretty good for someone who didn't even know what a bar mitzvah was when she started booking parties at a Sheraton Hotel in Minneapolis.

"If you're in corporate America and your career plan is to watch for job postings, you're not going to go very far, very fast," Vicki says. "Because by the time the jobs are posted, they're taken. You've got to identify a critical need the organization has and figure out if you're the person. If you can identify what that company needs and if you've got the skills to fulfill it, you're there."

Paying attention to what the company's goals are also means not getting caught up in the personalities you're working with—especially today when managers and leaders move around constantly. Vicki saw a lot of leadership changes in the two hotel companies where she spent most of her career, but she felt in control of her destiny because she was working toward the company's goals—not just her boss's.

As she neared the upper ranks, getting close to the president could be a liability—because when the president leaves, many of the upper executives often leave and follow him or her to the next job. If you're aware of the company's goals and how you fit into it, your job will be safer, she says.

"My allegiance has always been to the company as opposed to individuals," Vicki says. "For instance, I would never say that anybody in my department works for me. They don't work *for* me; they work for the company, and they *report* to me. I think that's a nuance that's lost on a lot of people. To me it's very, very important."

Be a team player who knows where upper-level management wants to take the company, Vicki says, and don't complain if the group decides not to take your advice every single time. "My personal philosophy is you pay me for my insight, my best advice, and my counsel. If you choose to not take it and choose to take a path that's not illegal, not immoral, or unethical, I will support it even though it's not the path I have said we should take. Either get on board or get off the bus."

Vicki admits she wasn't always this confident. In the beginning of her career, she wouldn't have even thought of taking the initiative to go after a job in the company that she wanted. But she had some great on-the-job learning.

Starting from Scratch

Vicki was a bright student who started college on an academic scholarship in her hometown of Clarksville, Tennessee. In her second year of school, she dropped out because her parents divorced, and her mother was responsible for Vicki, her younger brother and a sister who had Down syndrome. "This was in the late 1960s, and there weren't a lot of options for children with disabilities," Vicki explains.

"I was working, going to college, and helping care for my sister. I couldn't continue."

Eventually, she married a dashing young second lieutenant stationed in the 101st Airborne Division in nearby Fort Campbell, Kentucky. When he got out of the service, the couple moved back to his hometown of Minneapolis, where he went to school on the GI bill. "I had never lived in a big city," Vicki recalls, and even though the marriage didn't work out, you can hear in her voice that those were good years. "We were kids," she says with a laugh. It was the divorce that mad her look seriously at her own career. She found a job booking parties and banquets at the Minneapolis Sheraton, a smallish hotel in a great location by the airport.

"I had never been exposed to business before, and I absolutely loved it," Vicki says. "We were doing business with all these different companies. It was so cool." Right away she saw the advantage of the hotel industry: You meet all kinds of folks. In a lot of jobs, such as accounting or finance, "you're sort of doing the same thing every day," she says. "But when you're doing hospitality, you can talk to a pharmacy company and learn about that business, then you could sit down with someone and help them plan their wedding one day."

In other words, she loved the way her job exposed her to the world. "One of the first parties I planned was a bar mitzvah," she recalls. "I was from Clarksville, Tennessee. I didn't even know what a bar mitzvah was. It was great."

Another exciting aspect of the hospitality industry is the allure of travel. Every day Vicki would walk into the hotel and see gorgeous framed travel posters of other Sheraton hotels in exotic locations such as Rio and Paris. "I love to travel. I would see all those posters and say, 'I'm going to go there someday.'"

When Vicki left Sheraton, it was because she'd been offered a job at another Minneapolis hotel. It was a jump in pay and a bigger position—but she'd be soliciting sales, not just answering the phone to book and plan events. "I was really scared," she recalls. "I thought, 'I don't know if I can do that.' I remember having a conversation with a woman who was a sort of mentor for me at the time, and I said, 'They've offered me the job, but I don't think I can do this because I don't have a briefcase.' I remember her looking at me and saying, 'Buy a briefcase.'"

Vicki is self-assured and confident now, so it's funny to think of her being so full of self-doubt at her first step up the ladder, which just goes to show how quickly we can learn—and Vicki was a quick learner.

Underestimating Obstacles

Her new job at Ramada had a more corporate atmosphere than the Sheraton job—and being more corporate, the Ramada job had a clearly defined path for promotions. Vicki brought her briefcase to work and gained confidence in herself. She even earned a promotion to multilevel sales manager. She went from someone who saw obstacles everywhere—like not owning a briefcase—to someone who surmounted those obstacles.

These were also fun years. While working at Ramada, Vicki met her second husband, Bill, who was in the restaurant business. The two of them thought they had learned so much in their hospitality careers that between them they should be able to start their own business and get rich.

Vicki isn't the only person in this book who went out on her own and started a company. Starting your own business is, after all, part of the American Dream. My first book was all about people who have started their own companies rather than work for a corporation. But

Vicki's story also shows why I've written this second book—which is about how you can get the best of both worlds: the security of a job plus the excitement and advancement of entrepreneurship. Because running your own business is just plain tough.

In a nutshell, Vicki and her husband jumped out of corporate jobs—for a few years—and opened their own restaurant. That stint taught them something important. "The thing that Bill and I found was we liked the structure of corporate life," Vicki says. "We said, 'Man, we're working ourselves to death out here, and we are not making a whole lot of money. Let's go back to something we know.'" They were honest with themselves when things weren't working out, so they sold the restaurant and moved to suburban Chicago where she returned to Ramada.

This time, Vicki was regional director of field marketing at Ramada. She worked with all the hotels in a territory, pulled together all the franchise owners, and got them behind some of the corporate marketing efforts. She gathered the franchisees and presented them with opportunities to do co-op marketing, where the corporation would foot some of the bill but the franchisees had to kick in a share. Her territory was huge and included the Midwest and Northeast. But for someone who loves to travel and stay in nice hotels, it was a great job.

Working for the corporate side of things, Vicki learned a lot of inside information. One of the things she found out was that Ramada was about to be acquired by one of its own franchisees. This didn't sit well with Vicki, who knew the buyer and didn't want to work for him. "I didn't think I would fit in the new company culture," she says. "I wanted a change, I wanted a really stable environment," she recalls. "So I said, 'I want to go with the most stable hotels out there.'"

To her, that stable hotel would be Holiday Inn—and it just so happened that they had an opening in field marketing covering the Northwest.

Building Momentum—Assertively

But stability wasn't something to be found in the hotel industry. A month after joining Holiday Inn, the company announced it was being sold to Bass, a British beer brewer. Within 2 years the company moved its headquarters from Memphis to Atlanta, and Vicki followed. When she made the move, it was for a senior title: director of product marketing. Vicki's husband, who is older than her, was retired and moved with her to Atlanta.

Once she reached the title of director, Vicki started to see how competitive the upper ranks really are. This is the point in a career where a lot of people get frustrated—this is also where Vicki started to hone her philosophy of finding out what the company needed and identifying how she could fulfill that need.

It started when she was leading an ill-fated effort. "It was awful," Vicki recalls. "We were going to venture into electronic entertainment." Holiday Inn's new owner, Bass, also owned an electronic gaming machines business in the United Kingdom and thought it would be a good idea to have gaming centers at all the Holiday Inns. "They were convinced this was a huge opportunity," Vicki recalls. "It turned out to be a nightmare." Unfortunately, as vice president of new product development, the gaming project had been put under Vicki's leadership. "At some point I figured, 'This is going nowhere, and we are pouring money down a rat hole.'"

Vicki didn't want to go down with the ship, so she took the initiative to talk to her boss—even though they didn't have a great relationship. "I went to my boss and said, 'This isn't going to work, and I just cannot, as an officer of the company, see us going forward with this.' He said, 'I get your point. So what are you going to do?'"

Vicki was shocked. Her boss was leaving her out on a limb—but she swallowed her anger and thought to herself, "Well, clearly I'm not getting any help from you transitioning into anything else."

This was a situation that could be a career killer—you're tasked with something that's not working. Vicki's way of dealing with it was genius.

"There was no clear place for me to go," Vicki says. So she sat down with the company's business plan, looked at it, and thought, "There's got to be an opportunity for me here somewhere." She looked at all the things that were identified as critical to the company in the next 5 years. Then she looked at what kind of resources were being dedicated to meeting those goals. That's when she found it: Fostering communication in franchise relations was listed as a goal, but no one was really in charge of it.

So she went right to the president of the company and said, "I'd like to talk to you. I have a proposal. I realize you don't know me very well, but I've been with the company for a long time, and I've got a lot of history. I think we're vulnerable. I'll be perfectly candid with you. I'm looking for something I could pick up because I will be phasing out of this other effort. I think there's an area of need here, and I have the skill set to take this on. I would propose to you that you create this position and put me in it." He came back 3 days later and told her he thought she was right. The company created a new position for Vicki and put her in charge of communications between corporate and its franchises.

The moral of the story: "Find your opportunity," Vicki says. "Create your opportunity and go for it. Don't let somebody else determine your future. You've got to find that need that's not being served." Little did she know the challenges ahead.

Taking the Next Leap

When times are good, they're great. In the booming late-1990s, Vicki worked her way to the title of senior vice president of corporate affairs. There was a series of mergers and acquisitions, and the Holiday Inn brand became subsumed under the International Hotel Group (IHG) corporate name. That's when the going got tough.

In the downturn of late 2000, when technology industries crashed, the hotel industry was hit hard. One whole sector of American business was stalling out; struggling technology companies certainly didn't need conference rooms or hotel rooms. Then the September 11th terrorist attacks happened. "It had a devastating impact on our industry; you can't imagine," Vicki says. Vacancy rates fell through the floor, and revenues dropped by 50 percent across the board at all the hotel corporations. "It wasn't just in the United States. We saw that everywhere. We had this whole lockdown mentality. Travel came to a standstill."

Yet, just 2 days after September 11th, Vicki used the same philosophy for her company as she had used for her career: find the need. "We were going crazy trying to account for everybody," Vicki says. "We couldn't get a hold of people in New York. Cell phones weren't working. It was just chaos." In the midst of this crisis, Vicki saw there was a need for IHG to step up and help: The company should give $1 million to the Red Cross to aid in disaster relief efforts. At first her boss thought she was nuts. They didn't have that kind of money in the budget to donate, but she persevered. "I said, 'I have a plan,' and I sat down and laid out a plan for how I thought we could get there." Her plan included soliciting corporate donations from IHG's business partners, offering customers the ability to convert their Priority Club rewards points into cash donations to charity, collecting donations from their franchisees, and in-kind donating hotel rooms for rescue workers. The company might not have an extra $1 million lying around, but it had plenty of resources to help raise the funds.

When she showed the plan to the company president, he asked, "Do you honestly think we can do this?" She said, "Yes." He said, "Do it."

"Philanthropy is an important part of American culture," Vicki says. She knew deep in her bones that the Holiday Inn brand, which made up the bulk of IHG's holdings in the U.S., needed to step out and identify itself as part of the solution. "People in this country have such a strong feeling for the Holiday Inn brand. It would have been wrong if we hadn't done something," she says.

As other disasters hit, the model Vicki put into motion was brought out again and again. When the tsunami hit Sri Lanka, IHG stepped up again to raise money to help. And not only with rescue and relief, but also to help sustain the travel industry on the island. IHG kept long-term employees on the payroll, even when there were no jobs for them. They did the same after Hurricane Katrina hit New Orleans.

Vicki and her staff also came up with IHG's Designs of Hope, which is a gala of fundraising events held each spring in U.S. cities where IHG has hotel properties. In 5 years, the events raised $5 million for UNICEF, the United Nation's children's fund.

Looking back, Vicki says her hotel industry career "has been fabulous." She recommends her career strategy—finding a need at your company that you can fulfill—to up-and-coming executives. It's led her on a successful path in an industry she loves.

"I feel like I'm successful because my definition of success is being satisfied with where you are," Vicki says. "And I feel good about that."

As Vicki says, if you can find a need that you can fulfill in your company, you're there. Look at your own company or a company you'd like to work for, see where you could offer solutions, and see where it takes you.

Wes's Worry Less Tip

► **Solve today's problem today.**

When you know you're in a situation like Vicki Gordon was—where you know the future is bleak because you're assigned to a failing project—it would be easy to get caught up in worry. Instead of brooding, solve today's problem today. From a business point of view, finding solutions is the difference between those who make it—and those who don't. For your psyche finding a solution to today's problems is just plain mental therapy!

Even if you haven't found the right solution today, by taking *some* course of action—at least you're moving forward. By looking at the problem and putting energy into working toward a solution, you are taking a powerful step to clearing your mind over which direction to go. I'm much more calm and more productive once I'm working toward a goal, rather than waffling over which course of action to take. Some people spend half of their lives wondering *what if* and second guessing themselves. This just leads to added worry. If your first solution isn't perfect, you can always tweak it along the way. Put your energy into the solution instead of into worry, and tomorrow will take care of itself.

"Don't dwell on what went wrong. Instead, focus on what to do next. Spend your energies on moving forward toward finding the answer."

—Denis Waitley

18

Exercise Your Middle Brain

—Randy Brandoff (Marquis Jet)

Randy Brandoff is ambidextrous—he can comfortably perform most tasks with either his right or left hand. Pretty wild. I'm not suggesting that you need to be able to do this in order to be successful in business because if that's the case, I'm doomed. But Randy's story shows the strength of being adaptable rather than laser-focused. He calls it being *middle-brained*. Whatever you call it, Randy's ability to wear many hats launched him into a fantastic career as vice president of marketing at Marquis Jet, the industry leader in private jet cards.

Randy got started at Marquis Jet before it even had a name; in fact, he helped pick the name. He was the first employee, and his first few years on the job meant doing everything from figuring out financial models to buying media ads. "It's been all about wearing as many hats as you can try on," Randy says.

This is a refreshing point of view because so many people say you have to figure out what you're best at and pursue that. What if you don't have a laser focus? What if you're multitalented and pretty good at a wide range of things? There are people who can't figure out what they're best at, people who have a more broad level of competency. Randy calls it being "pretty good—to very good—at many things." He found a position and a company where that could be brought to its fullest value.

All along, even in college and his early working years, Randy had
this adaptable quality. First, he got a well-rounded business education
at Cornell University with a general business degree instead of specializing in a small field. At the same time, he did a couple of internships that seem to be from different sides of the planet: One summer
he played a young version of Charlie Sheen on *Wall Street* and the
next, Jerry Maguire's assistant at a talent agency. Then in his post-
college years, Randy worked first as a business analyst at Deloitte
Consulting and then as an associate for a venture capital firm. He was
immersed in analyzing business processes, but he wasn't tied to one
industry. When he talked with the founders of Marquis Jet, his adapt-
ability impressed them as just what they needed.

That's because when Marquis Jet got started, there was no estab-
lished path to follow. It was a totally new way of selling private air
travel. The way the Marquis Jet Card program works is customers
buy a jet card that's worth 25 hours of private flight time on the Net-
Jets fleet, sort of like a prepaid phone card, which can then be
redeemed over the following year.

When Randy met the Marquis Jet founders, they were hiring a
team that could get the business model off the ground. His wide-
ranging business experience made him just the right person for the
opportunity. "I've always said I'm not great at anything," says Randy,
who's being more than a little modest. "I have an understanding of a
wide gamut of things. I can be creative with advertising, print collateral, or designing a website, as well as analytical, crunching numbers
and building financial models. I have competency in a range of
areas."

Randy calls it being middle-brained. You know the theory: the
right and left hemispheres of our brains process information differently, and people tend to process information using their dominant
side. The left side of the brain is the calculating, analyzing, and math-
ematical side, whereas the right side is about creativity and flexibility.

In general, left-brained people are better at math and reading, whereas right-brained people are more artistic. Some people even think that because each hemisphere controls the opposite side of the body, being right-handed means you're left brain is dominant; left-handed means your right brain is dominant. When Randy says he's middle-brained, he means neither side is dominant—he's neither right- nor left-handed.

We don't have to change our brains to be successful—but we can make ourselves more flexible and adaptable. In fact, Randy tried on a couple of careers before he decided on marketing, and both times he was told he wasn't cut out for those jobs. So Randy adapted and tried something new.

Starting from Scratch

Majoring in business at Cornell University, Randy was on the freshman crew team, where he learned the importance of pulling his own weight. "You absolutely function and succeed as a team, and if one guy is messing up, you bring the entire boat down," Randy explains. "More than in any sport. Four guys can carry a bad basketball player, but when one guy's not in sync in your boat, the boat's going nowhere fast."

He also learned how to juggle diverging interests: he worked as a bartender for all 4 years of college, joined a fraternity, did some volunteering at a YMCA after-school program, and made good grades. Cornell's business program was very general; he focused on finance and marketing but also took classes in economics and other business disciplines.

His internships were a mixed bag as well—what I like to call an intern mogul of sorts. The first, the summer after freshman year, was with a family friend who was a trader on Wall Street. "I enjoyed it," Randy says, "but it wasn't my passion." Then, impressed with the

movie *Jerry Maguire,* which featured a hyper sports agent, Randy
spent two summers interning at talent agencies. While he was chatting with an up-and-coming actress one day, she looked at him and
asked, "What are you doing here? You're too smart for this place.
Why don't you try something more challenging? " Truthfully, Randy
saw that and agreed he needed a career that was less about "who you
know" and more about strategy and intellect.

Why not entertainment law? Again, he was discouraged. As he
was deciding between the law schools to which he'd been accepted,
his undergraduate law professor told him point blank: "Randy, I've
been doing this for 10 years, and I haven't seen many students that
sound less inclined to be a lawyer than you are. Take a year or two off,
get a job."

So Randy looked for a job and found an entry-level position as a
business analyst at Deloitte Consulting. There he found good executive training: the fundamentals of business, how to overcome barriers,
and how to motivate people. His first big project for Deloitte was at
Prudential Healthcare; the company was purchased by Aetna while
he was there. Randy recalls being fascinated to see how different people at Prudential handled the news. He watched as certain people
viewed it as an opportunity, and others viewed it as the end of the
world. His next big project was for Lucent Technologies, where he
worked at the headquarters in Murray Hill, New Jersey. He was
working on the company's global Y2K compliance, but what he
remembers most was at age 23 he had the opportunity to lead work-
shops for middle- and upper-level executives in Paris and Beijing.

After 2 years at Deloitte, Randy used a search firm to look around
for a job at a venture capital firm. He found one at the Argentum
Group in Manhattan, a small firm with five full-time investment professionals working around the clock. They hired him to assist with the
excess deal flow. This was in the first half of 2000, when the stock
market was still hot and before the dot-com crash. Within a couple

months of his hiring, however, the rapid market descent had begun; in the year he was there, not a single new deal was done.

At Argentum, a number of times Randy researched and made an investment recommendation in support of a company, and the partners would say, "'Good work, but we're not going to do the deal,'" Randy says. "It almost always came down to valuations, and they were too high. A good investment is largely defined by what price you ultimately pay for the company. And back then if someone basically had a dollar and a dream, they were asking for millions of dollars in valuation." After a year of no deals, Randy saw the writing on the wall and started speaking with search firms to look for something else. That's when a search consultant introduced him to the founders of Marquis Jet, who at the time were described as "a bunch of smart, already successful entrepreneurs I want you to meet."

Randy was curious and went to the meeting.

My Favorite Churchill Quote

"A pessimist sees the difficulty in every opportunity; an optimist sees the opportunity in every difficulty."

Underestimating Obstacles

Just the week before he met the Marquis Jet folks, Randy had read an article about NetJets, a Berkshire Hathaway company that sells shares of private jets to corporations and individuals who want the convenience and myriad of benefits of a private jet but don't want to buy and maintain the entire aircraft. Randy didn't realize it ahead of time, but the Marquis Jet founders had already negotiated an exclusive agreement with NetJets and were building a business around it.

So he sat down with the Marquis Jet founders, who were calling the company Superstar Jet at the time, and they unveiled their plan in a 10-page PowerPoint presentation. "I thought the opportunity was enormous," Randy recalls. "I also saw the obvious risk of a startup, but I was 25 years old, and I always had in the back of my head the likelihood I would go back to school. So I said to myself, 'Let's do this for a year or two, and if it's unsuccessful it would make a great essay to get into business school.'"

The Marquis Jet founders saw that NetJets, the founder of fractional jet ownership and worldwide leader in private aviation, served corporations and individuals who required at least 50 hours per year of flight time—and fractional jet ownership required a multiyear contract. Marquis Jet would partner with NetJets to buy shares on an assortment of aircraft types and resell those commitments in single year, 25-hour blocks of time, expanding the potential market for world-class private aviation.

The way the business works is, Marquis Jet Card owners can book flights 24/7, with as little as 10 hours advanced notice, on the NetJets fleet of over 670 jet aircraft. Marquis Jet Cards start at $119,900 for 25 hours of flight time and are good for 1 year. That's about $5,000 per hour, and if that sounds steep to you, that's because there are only about 400,000 people in the whole country who have a high enough net worth to afford it. But for those folks, time is money, and a private jet saves lots of time in addition to maximizing productivity and relieving the stresses of commercial travel. And, unless you fly an awful lot, buying a fractional share or a fractional jet card, depending on your need, is much less expensive than buying and maintaining your own jet.

When Randy began at Marquis Jet, the founders were looking to build the right team to take the winning concept off the page and make it a reality. Randy initially focused on crunching forecasts and developing the original financial model. Simultaneously, the team was deciding on the right look and tone of the brand and devising initial strategies to identify and market to a very niche audience. These were big jobs requiring diverse skills—just the thing for a middle-brained guy like Randy to make important contributions.

Especially appealing to Randy were the founders themselves. Founders Kenny Dichter and Jesse Itzler, who were less than 10 years older than Randy, had most recently co-founded Alphabet City, a production and distribution company that sold sports CDs combining music and play-by-play voiceovers. When they sold their company to SFX Entertainment, the pair ended up taking a few private jet flights with SFX clients and realized that the market for leasing private jets was wide open and full of opportunity.

Another member of the founding team whom Randy had immediate respect for was Henry Schachar, an attorney and seasoned executive. Earlier in his career, Schachar had been president of Philipp Brothers Inc., the leading global trader of non-ferrous and precious metals, as well as agricultural and energy-related products. While Dichter and Itzler were trying to convince NetJets to give them the green light to begin the business, they brought Schachar on board to be their "gray hair" and steadying influence.

Randy admired all of the founders' exuberance and sense of fun in business—and their accomplishments. Plus, it didn't hurt that they had an alliance with NetJets, which was owned by Warren Buffet's Berkshire Hathaway. He figured at the very least, this would be the learning opportunity of a lifetime!

Building Momentum—Flexibly

When they talk about it today, no one is exactly sure who first suggested the name Marquis Jet, but the process was unforgettable. Randy, the company's first employee, spent 5 days straight brainstorming in a room with the four founders and a naming consultant. Halfway through the week, every inch of the conference room had pages tacked up with names they had brainstormed. They started to vote down some of the names and pull down some of the pages until only a handful were left. Then they decided among those.

"It was a great process," says Randy, who recalls being the one who threw out the name Marquis Jet, but others in the room remember suggesting it also. "Probably more than one of us called out the name and didn't hear the others say it." Marquis Jet, with its connotation of European nobility, gave an elegant touch to the brand.

Randy spent much of that whole first year in 2001/2002 working on branding the startup—attempting to execute the vision of the founders and the newest addition to the company's founding team and leadership, Ken Austin. Prior to joining Marquis Jet, Austin was senior vice president at the Seagram Beverage Company, responsible for U.S. sales, regional marketing, finance, and operations. As Marquis Jet entered its second year of operations, the headcount had grown large enough to support breaking into departments, and Randy joined Ken in building the marketing and business development team.

His middle-brained flexibility came into play as the business grew. Randy worked hard to learn and successfully perform the functions that fell under his watch. He made it a point of pride that they were able to keep the team very lean and did not have to hire additional staff or outside agencies just because he didn't initially know how to do a particular job. They expanded the team only when they needed more manpower, or bandwidth. He learned a range of new tasks, including how to write press releases, draft new print ads, and lay out the content on the company's website.

One measure of Marquis Jet's initial marketing success that first year was when the Neiman Marcus winter catalog featured the Marquis Jet Card in its top five Christmas gifts for the season. That visibility helped lead to two other big early partners: the American Express Centurion Card and the Ritz Carlton Residence Club. As a startup, getting partnerships with well-known brands is an important way of gaining credibility. Thanks to its marketing techniques, Marquis Jet quickly gained that credibility.

A lot of people have trouble adapting to a chaotic environment, with so many hats to wear each day. For instance, in a job like Randy's, you might start out the day negotiating ad prices with a magazine, then finish the day designing a webpage promoting a new alliance partnership. But if you can be adaptable, you increase your value to the company.

No one on the founding Marquis Jet team had an aviation background. From day one they sought to create a world-class luxury brand that happened to sell an aviation product, rather than your typical jet company. Austin and Randy noticed that aviation marketing and advertising was previously all about the airplanes. They knew the primary driver to buying the Marquis Jet Card is that it enables busy people to get more time for their top priorities and to spend less time in airports. A Boston-based advertising agency gave them initial ad concepts for a groundbreaking lifestyle campaign, and the team has run with it. "Our current lifestyle campaign looks to touch an emotional trigger. Instead of talking solely about the product, we focus on the benefits," he says. Recent Marquis Jet ads use the tagline "It's not just a card, it's a choice." A choice, for example, to visit three cities each day and get home in time to celebrate your daughter's birthday. These ads have been successful.

"We definitely moved the ball," Randy says. "Now a lot of aviation ads are lifestyle-oriented. Our advertising changed the private aviation advertising landscape."

He knows the ads were successful because of the tracking engine they put into place from day one. "If you're going to have finite dollars for marketing and advertising, you're going to have to be as smart as possible," Randy says. At Marquis Jet, every different lead source—print ad, mailing, alliance partnership—has its own phone number. "Whenever a lead comes in, we know where they came from," Randy says, "so we know what's working up to the minute."

Taking the Next Leap

When people visit Marquis Jet's offices, the first thing they notice is the small staff. "We often hear people tell us, 'I see you guys everywhere, everyone knows you! You must have dozens of people working on it.'" And then they learn it's primarily Austin and Randy's marketing team. Then they look at the size of the team, which also manages the company's public relations and maintains the look and feel of the website, the print collateral, and the branding activity. "We have only a handful of people working on it," Randy says. Randy is quick to stress that the marketing team is able to accomplish what it does because every colleague, or teammate, is exceptionally talented and extremely hard-working. And Austin taught Randy how important it is to stretch a dollar intelligently, how to make a young business look bigger than it is. Looking big early on helped them form great alliances with big names, but staying small continues to help them keep a healthy bottom line.

But Marquis Jet isn't just about doing more with less—they want to do things in marketing that haven't been done before. For instance, Marquis Jet was the first corporate sponsor of *The Apprentice*. Back in 2004, for the show's first season, Marquis Jet was featured in *The Apprentice*'s second episode when the competing teams of contestants had to develop new promotional campaigns for the company. Marquis Jet provided flights from New York to Boston for the winning contestants. The show got the Marquis Jet name out there on national television, but it was a risk because at the time they agreed to participate, no one knew what the show would be like, and sponsors don't want to be associated with flops. What were people going to think of Donald Trump? Because the show was unproven, the price of Marquis Jet's participation was reasonable. However, it wasn't long before the show became a mega, international hit and began commanding millions for its advertising partnerships. So needless to say, the risk for Marquis Jet paid off in an enormous way. To this day, years later, not a week goes by that Randy doesn't hear, weren't you the company on *The Apprentice*?

Marquis Jet has also tried to be unique with its targeted advertising. Austin and Randy came up with the idea of running a targeted newspaper insert campaign. "We really got out there and did the research," Randy says. "We spent a number of months picking out the top 40 markets, then the top newspapers in each market, and the top 10 to 15 zip codes each selected newspaper reached." Armed with a list of the best newspapers and best zip codes, Randy's marketing team designed an eight-page insert, and Marquis Jet paid to have the inserts folded into those targeted newspapers. "Over 4 months we put 1.9 million inserts into the hands of potential high-net-worth consumers throughout the country," he says. It cost only a fraction of what it would have been to print brochures and mail them out to the same audience—less than 24 cents per piece instead of $15!

The brochure effort was something that had never been done before in aviation, Randy says, and it resulted in hundreds of quality leads and many sales.

After 6 years at Marquis Jet, Randy still loves it. "From day one through today, it's been amazing," he says. Even though he has thought of going out on his own and doing something entrepreneurial, now isn't the time. "As long as I can continue to be personally challenged and find myself growing and learning from the best, I'm staying," he says. "This is not a ride to jump off of anytime soon."

Middle-Brain Fitness

It's not enough anymore to jut use the left or right part of your brain. If you are going to reach your true potential at work, mental fitness is a key. Just like Randy, see if you are doing the following to keep your brain in shape.

- **Keep up with what's going on in the world.** Educate yourself and read voraciously! Set aside time to read articles on a wide variety of subjects. Try to read at least one book a month on a new subject. Successful people know what's happening in the business world, even if it doesn't directly apply to them. It's that simple, so get a subscription to the *Wall Street Journal* or, better yet, set your self apart with the *Financial Times*.

- **Build a network.** Volunteer in the community and attend civic groups such as Rotary or your local business associations. They are always looking for speakers, so volunteer to give a presentation about the most exciting thing happening in your industry!

- **Pick the brains of others.** Learn from your boss *and* your peers. If they know something you don't, it's a learning opportunity for you—not something to feel inferior about.

Left-, Right-, or Middle-Brained?

Here's a fun exercise (I'm not sure if it's strictly scientific) to check which side of your brain is dominant. With both eyes open, point at something far away from you. Then close one eye at a time and determine which eye matches up your finger with the point. If it's the left eye, you're more right-brained; if it's the right eye, you're more left-brained.

For more information on Wes speaking at your company, visit www.wesmoss.com.

Wes's Worry Less Tip

▶ **Minimize what you commit to memory.**

I've never known a scatterbrain who seems to be calm and in control. When we have too many things on our minds, we're like an overloaded computer processor: we shut down. Just like a computer that can run only two or three programs at a time and still process efficiently; our brains start to shut down when we try to keep more than a few things in our attention at once. We don't have enough attention or processing speed to do five things at once! Yet on any given day, most of us are working on several items at the same time, and we worry about losing track of any number of them.

Instead of relying on your memory and stressing yourself, get into the habit of living by a written schedule. A day in the life of Randy Brandoff is highly intense and complex; he has to be effective wearing a multitude of different "hats." On any given day he could be rewriting a script for product placement on the next episode of *Entourage*, negotiating an ad deal with a magazine, or working on a corporate alliance for Marquis Jet. To keep it all straight, he subscribes to Albert Einstein's philosophy: The more you have to remember, the more cluttered your mind becomes. Randy keeps his mind uncluttered by writing down his schedule and obligations. This way, he doesn't worry about what he's forgetting because he's already written it down.

*"The reason why worry kills more people than work
is that more people worry than work."*

—Robert Frost

Conclusion

Hopefully this book has helped you understand what it means to have the entrepreneurial mindset and learn how to HUNT. Most people tell me when they apply the HUNT principles to their careers they have a light-bulb moment of "Of course!" Succeeding financially isn't an either/or proposition. We're not living with two black-and-white choices: Business founders who strike it rich with money-making companies or peons who work for the business owners. If we consciously work at it, we can have the best of both worlds by leveraging our talents and choosing our employers well. However, sometimes we get so caught up in our responsibilities and failures that we forget that we *do* have control.

There's a direct relationship between control and worry; people who feel in control of their destiny don't have as many worries as those who feel like victims. Having an attitude of ownership at any size company—large or small—gives *you* the control. Control equals freedom, and freedom equals time, and time equals choice. So take the 18 lessons in this book, put as many of them into action as possible, and enjoy a life with less worry. It's not enough to make more money; what's the point of more money if you're hopped up all the time and worried sick. Remember, you have more control over your career than you think—you *can* have more of whatever you want, whether that's more time or more freedom—while worrying less.

Before you turn the last page of this book, I want to reiterate the importance of living within your means and staying out of debt. There is a lot of advice about how to do this, but it mainly comes down to paying out less than you bring in. Even though the goal of this book is to help you bring in more cash, be careful that you don't keep expanding your lifestyle with every bonus and every raise. If you're in debt now, use your raises and bonuses to get out of debt and stay there.

When you reach that point, consider it your baseline lifestyle, and use that new income to invest in the future or stash it away for a rainy day.

That way, you can take the risk on a new job or career—and if it doesn't work out you won't be bankrupt 2 weeks after you lose your job. You'll sleep a lot better at night if you have a financial cushion. If you're in debt, go without new things—for a little while—until you get that reserve built up.

Don't get me wrong: I think scrimping and saving are overrated. Most people could use a little scrimping, but they could also stand to increase their income. All the coupon-clipping in the world isn't going to give you a raise. Go ahead and watch your expenses, but then go out and leverage your talents, and increase your income. If you do that, you *will* build wealth.

After all, watching expenses and increasing income are what business owners do. You can do it too. We all want the combination of money, freedom, and corporate security that the entrepreneurial mindset offers.

Right now, as you set out to actively manage your career, imagine where you want to be at certain ages in the future. You can do this at any age: It works if you're in your 20s or 50s or beyond. Picture what you want and when you want it. Age-based goal setting is a great way to keep ourselves on task.

The HUNT isn't about coming up with a great idea; it's about the execution of great ideas. The word *entrepreneur* comes from the French for "to undertake." You can undertake the management of your career. And you do this by executing ideas—not coming up with them. How many people are going to come up with delivery pizza? Or new software? But we can all leverage our talents to help execute the great ideas behind all those companies out there. All it takes is using your skills and interests and optimistically and energetically applying yourself to execute those great ideas. It's simple, but it's not easy. You can use the entrepreneurial mindset to move forward—starting with today.

Wes's Worry Less Tip

For more regularly updated Worry Less Tips, visit www. wesmoss.com.

► Belief conquers worry.

I believe the most powerful force within you is your ability to believe. Everything else aside, if we believe we can do something, we can. Likewise, if we believe we can't, we're already defeated. So we might as well believe in ourselves and visualize what we want. If you really believe that you can do something or make something happen, then you can let go of worry and doubt. Recently a book entitled *The Secret* topped the bestseller lists with the message that anything that you desire in the world can be yours by using the the "secret." The "secret" itself refers to the "law of attraction," which essentially states that what you desire and focus on most intently will manifest through you—you will attract what you think about and what you focus on the most. Focus on negatives, and the universe will give you negatives. Focus on the positive things that you want, and they will be yours.

What I like about *The Secret* is its message of believing and focusing on outcomes before they happen and believing so wholeheartedly that you know the outcome is going to happen. Whether you believe in the metaphysical part of it or not, you can't argue with the power of knowing exactly what you want— and the belief that you are *going* to make it happen.

Part of living toward a goal is that in every second of the day, your psyche is working toward the accomplishment of that goal. If all you want in the world is to one day become a CEO, or to make a million dollars in a year, or to have your own television show, or to publish your own book, or to have a happy, loving family, then all of your thoughts and actions can work toward those things in every waking moment of the day. If you are in close touch with your deepest desires and goals in life, then there's a damn good chance it's going to happen. No matter how many obstacles there are between you and your goal, if you really want it badly enough—where you can literally see yourself at the head of the board room table or on stage talking about your latest book—you're going to seize upon opportunities and make the steps happen. If you really have faith that your efforts will ultimately bear fruit, then you'll constantly move forward to make your goals happen, instead of getting bogged down by obstacles. There's nothing more powerful than believing and knowing that things are going to work out as you wish.

"Pray as if everything depends upon God, then work as if everything depends on you."

—Martin Luther

INDEX